The Inclusive Classroom

"The book entitled, *The Inclusive Classroom: Creating a Cherished Experience through Montessori*, beautifully embraces the gift of a Montessori education while updating the curriculum to address the issues that impact the modern classroom. Each chapter examines a different component of a Montessori education while addressing the current curricular standards which guide our collective practice and acknowledges the needs of all learners. Humbly, the authors attend to the essence of a Montessori education while offering suggestions to meet the needs of diverse learners while respecting the child's learning and opportunity for growth." —**Kathleen G. Winterman**, director, School of Education, College of Professional Sciences, Xavier University, Cincinnati, Ohio

"*The Inclusive Classroom: Creating a Cherished Experience Through Montessori* provides insight into the direct link between Montessori, Universal Design for Learning (UDL), and meeting the needs of all learners, including those with disabilities. It supports teachers with clear lessons, examples, and suggested adaptations to foster an environment that promotes the philosophy of Maria Montessori through a contemporary lens that adheres to the National Association for the Education of Young Children standards." —**Catherine Lawless Frank**, EdD, assistant professor, special education, School of Education and Health Sciences: Teacher Education, University of Dayton, Dayton, Ohio

"*The Inclusive Classroom: Creating a Cherished Experience through Montessori* demonstrates the effectiveness of a dynamic pedagogy whose curriculum and facility for differentiated instruction puts the child at the center while encouraging engagement, connection-making and concept mastery according to the child's needs. All early childhood practitioners can benefit from the conscious links of Montessori curricula and methodology to the NAEYC standards and the Universal Learning Design framework in this clearly written guide to meeting the needs of young learners in an inclusive early childhood classroom community. The reference to specific curriculum lessons enhanced by case study examples makes this a suitable handbook for teacher education students as well as new and experienced early childhood practitioners." —**Gay C. Ward**, PhD, professor emerita of literacy, child development and Montessori studies, University of Wisconsin-River Falls

The Inclusive Classroom

Creating a Cherished Experience through Montessori

Ginger Kelley McKenzie, Victoria S. Zascavage,
Vanessa M. Rigaud, Crystal Dahlmeier,
and My Le N. Vo

With Special Contribution by Laura Saylor

ROWMAN & LITTLEFIELD
Lanham • Boulder • New York • London

Published by Rowman & Littlefield
A wholly owned subsidiary of The Rowman & Littlefield Publishing Group, Inc.
4501 Forbes Boulevard, Suite 200, Lanham, Maryland 20706
www.rowman.com

6 Tinworth Street, London SE11 5AL, United Kingdom

Copyright © 2021 by Ginger Kelley McKenzie, Victoria S. Zascavage, Vanessa M. Rigaud, Crystal Dahlmeier, and My Le N. Vo

All rights reserved. No part of this book may be reproduced in any form or by any electronic or mechanical means, including information storage and retrieval systems, without written permission from the publisher, except by a reviewer who may quote passages in a review.

British Library Cataloguing in Publication Information Available

Library of Congress Cataloging-in-Publication Data

Names: McKenzie, Ginger Kelley, author. | Zascavage, Victoria S., author. | Rigaud, Vanessa M., author. | Dahlmeier, Crystal, author. | Vo, My Le N., author.
Title: The inclusive classroom : creating a cherished experience through Montessori / Ginger Kelley McKenzie, Victoria S. Zascavage, Vanessa M. Rigaud, Crystal Dahlmeier, and My Le N. Vo.
Description: Lanham : Rowman & Littlefield, [2021] | Includes bibliographical references.
Identifiers: LCCN 2020057011 (print) | LCCN 2020057012 (ebook) | ISBN 9781475856347 (cloth) | ISBN 9781475856354 (paperback) | ISBN 9781475856361 (ebook)
Subjects: LCSH: Montessori method of education. | Inclusive education. | Special education.
Classification: LCC LB1029.M75 M42 2021 (print) | LCC LB1029.M75 (ebook) | DDC 371.39/2—dc23
LC record available at https://lccn.loc.gov/2020057011
LC ebook record available at https://lccn.loc.gov/2020057012

This book is dedicated to all children, including children with challenges. It is also dedicated to all teachers, parents, and friends who see the world in all its created glory—and who therefore show compassion, love, and caring energy toward all children.

—Ginger Kelley McKenzie, EdD

Contents

Foreword *Laura Saylor*		xiii
Preface *Ginger Kelley McKenzie and Victoria S. Zascavage*		xv
Acknowledgments *Ginger Kelley McKenzie*		xix
1	Introducing Montessori Inclusive Education *Ginger Kelley McKenzie and Victoria S. Zascavage*	1
	Overview of the National Association for the Education of Young Children (NAEYC)	3
	Overview of Universal Design for Learning (UDL)	5
	Notes	8
	Bibliography	11
2	Practical Life *My Le N. Vo*	15
	Dr. Montessori's Pedagogical Principles and NAEYC Information	16
	What Are the Purposes of Practical Life Lessons?	18
	What Are the Areas of Practical Life Activities?	18
	A Touch of Cultural Diversity	22
	How Do Practical Life Activities Benefit Children in an Inclusive Classroom?	22
	Teacher Observations	23

	A Deepened Awareness	24
	Strengthened Perspectives	25
	Notes	26
	Bibliography	27
3	Montessori Sensorial Lessons *Crystal Dahlmeier*	29
	Keys to the Intellect	29
	Sensitive Period for Sensation	30
	Qualities of the Lessons	31
	The Guide	31
	From Concrete to Abstract	33
	Sequential Learning	34
	Introduction of Language	35
	Variations and Extensions	37
	Summary	41
	Notes	42
	Bibliography	43
4	Early Childhood Montessori Mathematical Education *Ginger Kelley McKenzie and Victoria S. Zascavage*	45
	Practical Life and the Pouring Activity	49
	Sensorial Preparation and Dimensional Activities	50
	Number Ordering	51
	Three Period Lesson Format and Relationship to Direct Instruction	52
	Counting: Montessori Methods of Instruction	53
	Number Rod Activity	53
	Sandpaper Numeral Activity	56
	Number Rods and Smooth Numeral Cards	58
	Spindle Box Activity	60
	Red Wooden Counter Activity or Numerals and Counters	60
	Geometry Concepts	61
	Geometric Shapes—Three-Dimensional Geometric Solids	62
	Flat Geometric Shapes	64
	Constructive Triangle Boxes	66
	Mathematics and the Inclusive Classroom	74

	Summary of Math Strategies for Supporting Children with Learning Challenges	76
	Notes	77
	Bibliography	80
5	Montessori Language Practices Meet the Needs of All Learners	83
	Vanessa M. Rigaud	
	Montessori Holistic Language Program for Early Childhood Children	84
	Early Preparations for Language Development for All Children	86
	Exercises for the Hand: Fine Motor Preparation for Writing	90
	Exercises for Phoneme, Graphemes, and Correspondence Preparation	92
	Exercises for Reading	95
	Early Language and Literacy Adaptations and Alignment	98
	Notes	100
	Bibliography	102
Conclusion		103
Ginger Kelley McKenzie and Victoria S. Zascavage		
	Practical Life Chapter	104
	Sensorial Chapter	105
	Math Chapter	107
	Language Chapter	108
Appendix		111
About the Authors		117

Foreword

"But aren't you a Montessori teacher? Wasn't Montessori first developed for children with special needs?"

Early in my teaching career, these questions were posed to me by a parent of a child with some learning challenges. The child was in my early childhood classroom, and I had told the parent that I was not sure my Montessori classroom could meet the child's needs.

I had been teaching for a few years, and I was pretty confident in my abilities. But this parent's questions had me reflecting on my Montessori training and preparation and on my own understanding of teaching children with special needs. I wondered why I did not feel prepared to work with this student.

I was well aware of Montessori's history of working with children who have special needs and how it served as a basis for her method. I had been well trained to teach early childhood education in a Montessori classroom; I had a state teaching license and a certificate in Montessori Education. Perhaps, as a Montessorian, I felt I should know more about working with this student and others. Here began my serious exploration of inclusion in Montessori early childhood environments.

Little did I know at that time that I would spend decades considering, studying, and developing inclusive teaching practices in and out of Montessori environments. As a Montessorian, I utilized my training as an observer of young children. A few years later, as a graduate student, I studied how to meet the needs of a diverse group of learners. I continued this journey as a school leader, where I learned from intervention specialists and experts about the needs of exceptional learners. Later, as a PhD candidate, I would immerse myself in the body of research regarding inclusion of children with special needs in general education classrooms. Here I learned the teaching practices in Montessori education were indeed supported by the literature. In fact, my fellow PhD candidates, after reviewing literature on an evidenced-based educational practice, would often turn to me and say, "Don't they already do that in Montessori?"

My journey continues to this day. As the dean of a school of education, I have learned much about preparing student educators to be inclusive in their teaching practices. My journey in learning about and implementing evidence-based practices in inclusive settings has been long and at times arduous. However, and in the end, what I came to learn is the same lesson that the Scarecrow, the Tin Man, and the Cowardly Lion came to learn in *The Wizard of Oz*. I learned that, as a trained Montessori educator, I already possessed the roots that I was searching for. What I really needed was to dig deeper into my understanding of Montessori and nourish what I would find there with intentional and persistent growth as an educator.

That is the reason I am so enthusiastic about the publication of this book. This book will allow Montessori educators to more easily identify and implement those inclusive teaching practices that are essential components of Dr. Maria Montessori's method.

The authors have carefully laid out the case for Montessori as an inclusive teaching method in each area of the early childhood prepared environment. They have done the work of aligning Montessori practices and lessons with the standards of NAEYC and the principles of Universal Design for Learning. Additionally, the authors have illustrated through examples exactly how Montessori education is, at its core, an inclusive method developed by the scientific and intentional design of Dr. Maria Montessori.

I wish all the best to you on your journey as an inclusive Montessori educator. I hope you will find this book to be an informative guide during the extraordinary adventure upon which you have embarked.

Laura Saylor, PhD
School of Education, Mount St. Joseph University

Preface

Creating a Cherished Experience: The Montessori Early Childhood Inclusive Classroom

Ginger Kelley McKenzie and Victoria S. Zascavage

This book is the collaborative effort of five experts in Montessori Education and Special Education (for 3- to 6-year-old children) in Montessori schools. Predominantly, this book is for Montessori professionals but also can serve as a textbook for teacher-training programs at the undergraduate and graduate levels. The chapters are for Montessori teachers in public, private, sectarian, and religious school classrooms for ages 3 to 6, as well as for Montessori administrators.

Each chapter in this book includes examples of specific instructions designed to enable educators in inclusive Montessori classrooms to adjust or re-present lessons for children with learning challenges. Each lesson design reflects the principles of Universal Design for Learning (UDL)[1] and the specific standards from the National Association for the Education of Young Children (NAEYC).[2] This book provides dedicated, caring Montessori teachers and Montessori teachers-in-training around the world with a practical resource for the instruction of children who have learning challenges as well as those children who need additional academic support.

The aim of this book is not so much to describe how materials function in the Montessori classroom but rather to describe the ways the materials and philosophy of Maria Montessori can be adapted to accommodate children with a variety of learning styles and social, emotional, and educational needs. Maria Montessori, a twentieth-century visionary, designed a program to educate students with intellectual disabilities. Because of the contemporary nature of our interpretation of Montessori, we have designed this book to use twenty-first-century expertise to accommodate students in early childhood Montessori classrooms. The methods and use of concrete, hands-on materials are not Montessori exclusive and are suited for incorporation into any traditional classroom that needs innovative instructional support in order for students to learn.

Specifically, we have recommended accommodations for traditional lessons on how to adjust or re-present these lessons to children with learning challenges. Each lesson adheres to the principles of UDL and the specific standards from the NAEYC and applies these to the Montessori areas of Practical Life, Sensorial, Mathematics, and Language Arts.

"Practical Life" (chapter 2) begins with children wanting to imitate adult activities. Through activities such as washing dishes, simple carpentry, and food preparation, children learn to respect materials, sequence activities, concentrate on a task, and appreciate order. The chapter is sensitive to the adaptations and extra support so often needed in an inclusive classroom to support an atmosphere of caring and learning where each child has the opportunity to participate as a cherished member of the group.

The Practical Life area of the Montessori Environment supports practical skills that will help the child with both direct and indirect learning. A cycle of activity helps the child internalize order while learning respect of the materials. Both gross and fine motor skills develop in this area with carefully designed activities sequenced in difficulty that actively engage each child. The activities in Practical Life help develop a community of learners who demonstrate a respect and compassion for all cultures.

"Montessori Sensorial" (chapter 3) presents a curriculum that Maria Montessori considered both scientific and mathematical. Using the sensorial materials, the child is able to identify, classify, seriate, and sequence information. The materials are naturally multisensory in order to accommodate a wide range of learning styles and abilities. The chapter includes examples of children who need additional support and the accommodations used by their teacher.

"Early Childhood Montessori Mathematical Education" (chapter 4) discusses the needs of the inclusive classrooms while following the educational standards of the NAEYC,[3] the Common Core State Standards Initiative,[4] and the tenets of the National Council of Teachers of Mathematics (NCTM).[5] This chapter blends NAEYC recommendations with the principles of UDL and Montessori educational pedagogy. The lessons in chapter 4 include examples of how to change or re-present lessons to support students who need additional academic support.

"Montessori Language Practices Meet the Needs of All Learners" (chapter 5) demonstrates Montessori's belief that language should develop organically when guided with the developmentally appropriate didactic materials. In Montessori, language development begins with the initial lesson in Practical Life. The teacher trains the child's ear with clear and precise speech that provides nomenclature related to the exercise, leaving out extraneous concepts.

Chapter 5 provides concrete strategies and lesson adaptations for effective teaching in the Montessori early childhood environment. It will serve as a guide in preparing Montessori lessons for a diverse group of learners in the area of language development and literacy.

The goal of an adapted Montessori curriculum is to welcome all students into a full Montessori experience. For the students who need additional support, the joy of education depends on a prepared environment designed to maximize their potential and participation. The foundational curriculum designed by Maria Montessori and adapted in this book employs concrete materials of beauty and purpose to engage all learners and create cherished experiences. Based on the pedagogy of Maria Montessori and modernized by the guidelines of the NAEYC and UDL, this book encompasses the perspective of its authors' many years of experience in Montessori early childhood and/or special education, who bring their expertise to chronicle the new Montessori normal.

NOTES

1. "Universal Design for Learning Guidelines" CAST, last modified 2020, www.cast.org/our-work/about-udl.html?utm_source=udlguidelines&utm_medium=web&utm_campaign=none&utm_content=homepage#.XngW0PZFw2w.

2. "NAEYC Standards for Early Childhood Professional Preparation," National Association for the Education of Young Children, 2009, last modified 2009, https://www.naeyc.org/sites/default/files/globally_shared/downloads/PDF/resource.

3. "Early Childhood Mathematics: Promoting Good Beginnings," NAEYC, 2002, last modified 2010, https://naeyc.org/files/NAEYC/file/positions?psmath,pdf.

4. "Kindergarten, Counting & Cardinality," Common Core State Standards Initiative, last modified 2020, http://www.corestandards.org/Math/Content/K/CC/.

5. "Principles and Standards for School Mathematics," National Council of Teachers of Mathematics, accessed January 15, 2018, https://www.nctm.org/standards-and-positions/principles-and-standards.

Acknowledgments

I am grateful to all of the authors and contributors who have shared their knowledge and passion for Montessori early childhood education and understanding of how to support children with challenges. I give thanks for their willingness to share their expertise with all those who read this book.

I owe an enormous amount of gratitude to Ann Sullivan who helped edit, format, and organize our manuscript. She is an excellent writer, and I am so lucky to have her as a great friend and neighbor.

And finally, I thank every parent, friend, and teacher who shows their love and compassion to all children on this glorious earth God has created for all of us. God's love, joy, and peace be with you and yours always.

Ginger Kelley McKenzie, EdD

Chapter One

Introducing Montessori Inclusive Education

Ginger Kelley McKenzie and Victoria S. Zascavage

Maria Montessori (1870–1952) was born August 31, 1870, in Chiaravelle near the Italian port city of Ancona on the Adriatic. She was an only child of parents of moderate means.[1] Montessori's accomplishments include graduating with a double major from the University of Rome in medicine and surgery. She was the first woman to get a medical degree in Italy. As described by Lillard,[2] Montessori developed her new philosophy of education based on her careful and extensive observation of children.

Montessori's philosophy of education was in the tradition of Jean Jacques Rousseau, Johann Heinrich Pestalozzi, and Friedrich Froebel. These scholars emphasized the innate potential of the child. Montessori also studied the educational methods of Edouard Sequin, a pioneer in the field of childhood education.[3] In 1904, she opened a preschool for children with intellectual disabilities.[4] Soon she established her first school for all children known as the "Casa dei Bambini" or House of Children.[5]

Montessori "was able to observe in slow motion, as it were, the sensitive periods that govern the development of the abnormal child, and she applied this knowledge to her later work."[6] Just as Freud began his psychological studies with troubled patients and used his findings to understand the general populous, Montessori began her educational study of children with intellectual disabilities and used it as a point of departure for understanding all children.[7]

Montessori's first visit to America was in 1913 and lasted a month.[8] Her methods of education, originally met with enthusiasm, gradually came to be faced with criticism.

American professionals like William Kilpatrick felt that her theory did not provide enough situations for social cooperation.[9] During Montessori's second visit in 1914, she presented a summer course at the Panama-Pacific Exposition in San Francisco, a celebration of the completion of the Panama Canal.[10] Montessori's last visit to the United States was in 1918 and was personal and unpublicized.[11]

When Montessori left America, she asked Helen Parkhurst to be in charge of the Montessori movement in the United States and to manage the National Montessori Promotion organization. However, Parkhurst soon decided to leave the organization and struck out on her own to establish the Dalton Laboratory Play School.[12]

A period of transition ended with the Montessori American Renaissance of the 1950s and 1960s. In 1958, under the leadership of Nancy McCormick Rambusch, the Whitby School opened in Greenwich, Connecticut, as the first Montessori school in the United States.

The Whitby School became the first location for the American Montessori Association. William Hopple visited the Whitby School and was so impressed that, in the early 1960s, he opened a Montessori school at Cincinnati Country Day School (CCDS) in Cincinnati, Ohio.

Hilda Rothschild, a Montessori teacher at CCDS had trained in France. She saw a need for a Montessori teacher-training center at Xavier University. In 1965, Dr. Raymond McCoy and Mike Morra opened the Montessori Training Center for graduate students at Xavier University.[13]

The American Montessori Renaissance in the 1960s was a reaction to the realization that a high numbers of children could not read, were dropping out of school, and were not being adequately challenged in school.[14] The movement gained support. Psychologist Dr. Donald Hebb supported Dr. Montessori's use of intrinsic motivation for learning. The San Francisco Montessori Head Start program provided evidence that preschool Montessori programs provided children a superior education at a lower cost.[15]

In 1967, David Elkind wrote in the *Harvard Educational Review*: "The Piagetian and Montessorian concepts in this county are gratifying and long overdue. . . . We need to accept their methods without distortion for our own pragmatic purposes."[16]

By 1974, there were 1,500 Montessori schools, most of which were private. By 1989, there were 110 public Montessori schools serving 14,000 children and 4,000 private Montessori schools.[17] Twentieth-century Montessori schools were predominantly private schools with very few accepting children with disabilities. Now, in the twenty-first century, there are 550 public and 2,139 private Montessori schools in the United States.[18]

The renewed Montessori inclusion initiative addressed issues of social justice and the mandates for inclusive education in the Every Student Succeeds Act of 2015 (ESSA), doing so in the least restrictive environment and to the greatest extent possible for all students with a disability.[19]

The American Montessori Society (AMS) has 110 teacher education programs, and the Association Montessori Internationale (AMI) has 92 teacher education programs, all affected by ESSA.[20] The inclusion momentum in Montessori spans schools in 36 different states in the United States and 21 international programs accredited by the AMS.[21]

The AMS offers credentialed teachers the option of adding a special-education endorsement to their licensure/credential.[22] Montessori worldwide is at the edge of total inclusion. There is a general recognition that the principles and pedagogy of Montessori education provide a good fit for students with disabilities.[23]

This book addresses best-practice accommodations to facilitate full inclusion in Montessori schools. Each chapter supports a blend of the NAEYC) Standards, Common Core Curriculum, Montessori philosophy and curriculum, and the principles of UDL. For those unfamiliar with NAEYC Standards and UDL, the following overviews will prove helpful.

OVERVIEW OF NAEYC

NAEYC, founded in Washington, DC, in 1926, published its first position statement on developmentally appropriate practices, serving young children in early childhood classrooms from birth to age 8.[24] In 1996, a revised and expanded edition of the 1986 NAEYC position statement "Basics of Developmentally Appropriate Practice: An Introduction for Teachers of Children 3 to 6" addressed the following major issues:

- the teacher as decision maker
- the importance of setting goals for children that are both challenging and achievable

- expanding the basic definition of developmentally appropriate practice to include
- consideration of social and cultural context[25]

The third edition of NAEYC's *Developmentally Appropriate Practice in Early Childhood Programs"* has four chapters:

- "The Infant and Toddler" (now a separate chapter)
- "The Preschool Years"
- "The Kindergarten Year" (now a separate chapter)
- "The Primary Grades"

Each chapter in the NAEYC manual gives an overview of the child's development and appropriate teaching practices for their social, academic, emotional, and physical well-being.[26]

In 2009, NAEYC adopted the current position statement, which includes the following in the "Guidelines for Developmentally Appropriate Practice":

- creating a caring community of learners
- teaching to enhance development and learning
- planning curriculum to achieve important goals
- assessing children's development and learning
- establishing reciprocal relationships with families[27]

NAEYC holds two national early childhood conferences each year. They publish periodicals, books, professional-development materials, and resources every year. In 1985, NAEYC began providing national accreditation for early childhood programs. Now, in 2020, they are one of the accreditation bodies granting licensure in early childhood teacher education.[28]

The math chapter in this book embraces the educational standards of the NAEYC and the tenets of the National Council of Teachers of Mathematics (NCTM). In a joint paper, NAEYC and NCTM determined ten research-based interventions recommended for early childhood mathematics.[29] Chapter 4 lists these intervention strategies and incorporates them into the math lessons described in the chapter.

Teaching strategies identified in this book connect directly to the principles proposed by outstanding NAEYC leaders in the early childhood education realm of the United States. In the appendix, Montessori 3–6 principles are integrated with sixteen NAEYC principles:

Prepared Environment
Observation
Order
Concentration
Freedom within Limits
Free Choice
Role of the Teacher
Limited Materials
Absorbent Mind and the Sensitive Periods
Self-correcting Materials
Development of Community
Initiative
Self-Discipline
Attachment
Meaningful Work and Independence
Movement

OVERVIEW OF UDL

Best-practice incorporation of UDL into curriculum planning and intervention is not new. UDL theory has been built into recommendations for implementation by several movements in educational reform: the Higher Education Opportunity Act of 2008,[30] the Every Student Succeeds Act of 2015,[31] and the National Education Technology Plan of 2016.[32]

Along with NAEYC and the tenets of Montessori 3–6 principles, UDL provides the tools to connect necessary accommodations to the practical and theoretical pedagogy that is Montessori. When instructional practices implement UDL, individuals with learning differences and disabilities are no longer subject to barriers limiting learning opportunities. The practice of UDL has the potential to maximize learning for all students by providing opportunities for rehearsal, application, and individualization.

UDL is a natural complement to Montessori methodology in both philosophy and practical implementation. UDL is an interpretation of curriculum that addresses three very important tenets of learning:

- affect networks
- strategic networks
- recognition networks

With these tenets as guidelines, access to learning becomes a flexible approach to teaching methods, materials used in practice and instruction, and the manner of assessment required from the individual student.[33]

Throughout this book, UDL principles and guidelines for implementation supplement most Montessori accommodations. For example, in the area of Practical Life, the Pouring Activity makes use of variation in materials to accomplish a pouring lesson in keeping with UDL Principle 1: Providing Multiple Means of Representation. This approach allows customization of the display of information as learning tool.[34]

In chapter 4 (mathematics), the guidelines of UDL Principle II: Provide Multiple Means of Action and Expression govern adaptations that offer options for physical action.[35] For example, Principle II advises the teacher to vary the methods for response and navigation to support accommodations. When applied to the Number Rod Activity for students with challenges, this principle varies the time and method needed to transport the rods, taking into account the need of individual students and their individual attention span, need for kinesthetic relief, and/or physical limitations.

The use of UDL Principle III: Provide Multiple Means of Engagement, Guideline 7, Checkpoint 7.1 suggests that students will benefit from optimized individual choice and autonomy.[36] For example, the ten trips to the math shelf normally needed to set up the Long Rod Activity may overwhelm challenged children because of the additional stamina or concentration required of them. In these cases, asking the student to make only three trips at a time is advisable. Offering the student choices and/or streamlining the requirements of the activity supports the student's success and has the added benefit of introducing the student to the concept of calm peace.

In 1979, Montessori pointed out that experiences in the Practical Life area build a child's natural interest, positive work habits, concentration, attention span, and body control because they teach the basic principles of volume and conservation. She refers to this as the ability to "move about under the guidance of reason . . . in a deliberate and thoughtful manner . . . that is the mark of inner discipline which manifests itself in orderly, external acts."[37]

According to Dr. Montessori, "Offering learners choices can develop self-determination, pride in accomplishment, and increase the degree to which they feel connected to their learning."[38] Free choice allows children to take material that corresponds to their "own inner needs" and allows teachers to observe the concentration and provide order that is proportional to the child's use, interest, and maturity.

Montessori education provides an environment tailored to include most students with disabilities. The decision of suitable placement in public schools and/or private Montessori schools depends upon determining which environment is least restrictive. Least-restrictive-environment decisions are made with the intention that "removal of children with disabilities from the regular educational environment occurs only if the nature or severity of the disability is such that education in regular classes with the use of supplementary aids and services cannot be achieved satisfactorily."[39]

Montessori materials provide opportunities for children to access and express their learning in a unique way. This individualization of learning and its expression also reflect the UDL concept of offering the child multiple means of representation, expression, and engagement. Montessori teachers tailor instruction to the needs of the child, thus creating a least restrictive environment. As stated by Jacqueline Cossentino, "In a foundational way, then, Montessorians are, at the very least, close cousins of special educators."[40]

The Individual with Disabilities Education Act (IDEA)[41] guarantees individualized educational instruction to public school students with disabilities. Individualized instruction is very similar to the Montessori concept of "follow the child."[42] For example, opportunities for choice and extended periods of deep concentration combined with free movement are "pillars of Montessori pedagogy" and are simultaneously best-practice strategies for educating a student with attention deficit disorder.[43]

David Kahn, editor for the North American Montessori Teachers Association (NAMTA) special edition periodical "The Holistic Meaning of Inclusion in Montessori Education" states:

> Montessori education must fully explore inclusion as a pervasive and complex approach to meeting the needs of all children: non-neurotypical, gifted, typically developing, children who have experienced trauma, and children of various ages, stages, and capabilities within the same classroom.[44]

Successful inclusion depends on a well-designed program that provides optimum academic and social skills for the student with learning challenges.[45] Inclusion is not a placement but a process of supportive best practices provided in an effective learning environment. An inclusive curriculum welcomes all learners to explore and engage with the materials and the lesson. Inclusion offers additional support for independence, variation on methods of assessment, and individualized direct instruction when necessary.

Optimally, inclusion is a way to serve the needs of all learners within a classroom setting that respects the unique learning styles and personal differences of all students. Maria Montessori based her pedagogy on maximizing educational opportunity for all children. Today, the triad of physical, social, and instructional inclusion emerges as the foundation upon which the Montessori inclusive classroom is built, allowing it to serve the needs of all children.

NOTES

1. Reginald Orem, *Montessori: Her Method and the Movement: What You Need to Know* (New York: G. P. Putman's Sons, 1974), 245.
2. Paula Lillard, *Montessori: A Modern Approach* (New York: Schoken Books, 1972), 29.
3. Orem, *Montessori*, 248.
4. Lena Gitter, *The Montessori Way* (Seattle: Special Child Publication, 1970), 9.
5. Orem, *Montessori*, 250.
6. Gitter, *The Montessori Way*, 9.

7. Rita Kramer, *Maria Montessori: A Biography* (Chicago: University of Chicago Press, 1983), 373.

8. Lee Deighton, "Maria Montessori," *Encyclopedia of Education* (New York: Macmillan, 1971), 389.

9. Lillard, *Montessori*, 10.

10. Kramer, *Maria Montessori*, 209.

11. Orem, *Montessori*, 251.

12. Ibid.

13. Deighton, "Maria Montessori," 390.

14. Edwin Standing, *The Montessori Revolution in Education* (New York: Schocken Books, 1966), 196.

15. Orem, *Montessori*, 159.

16. David Elkind, "Piaget and Montessori," *Harvard Educational Review* 18, no. 2 (1967): 543.

17. David Cohen, "Public Schools Embrace Montessori Movement," *Education Week* 9, no. 15 (1989): 2.

18. "Montessori Census," Montessori Census, accessed March 25, 2020, https://www.montessoricensus.org.

19. Every Student Succeeds Act, US Department of Education, accessed March 15, 2018, https://www.ed.gov/essa.

20. "Number of Montessori Teacher Education Programs," Montessori Census, accessed March 25, 2020, https://www.montessoricensus.org.

21. "Inclusion Momentum in Montessori A.M.S. Accredited Programs," National Center for Montessori Education in the Public Sector, accessed March 1, 2020, https://www.public-Montessori.org.

22. "About Montessori. Montessori for Children with Special Needs," American Montessori Society, accessed April 2, 2020, https://www.amshq.org/About-Montessori/Montessori-for-Children-with-Special-Needs. Has endorsement for special education.

23. Natalie Danner and Susan Fowler, "Montessori and Non-Montessori Teacher's Attitudes Towards Inclusion and Access," *Journal of Montessori Research* 1, no. 1 (2015): 29–41; Ginger McKenzie and Victoria Zascavage, "A Model for Inclusion in Early Education Classroom," *Montessori Life* 24, no. 1 (2012): 32–38; Joyce A. Pickering, "Montessori for Children with Learning Differences" *Montessori Life* 28, no. 2 (2017): 49–53.

24. Carol Copple and Sue Bredekamp, eds. *Developmentally Appropriate Practice in Early Childhood Programs Serving Children from Birth through Age 8*, third edition (Washington, DC: National Association for the Education of Young Children, 2017), viii.

25. Copple and Bredekamp, *Developmentally Appropriate Practice*, viii.
26. Ibid., 16–23.
27. "About NAEYC Membership," National Association for the Education of Young Children, 2011/a, accessed April 16, 2019, https://www.naeyc.org/content/about-naeyc.
28. "About NAEYC Membership." National Association for the Education of Young Children, accessed April 16, 2019, https://www.naeyc.org/content/about-naeyc. 2011/a.
29. "Early Childhood Mathematics Promoting Good Beginnings," National Association for the Education of Young Children, last modified 2010, https://www.NAEYC.org/files/NAEYC/file/positions/psmath.pdf.2002,2010,3.
30. H.R. 4137 Higher Education Opportunity Act, 110th Congress, 2007–2008, accessed April 17, 2020, Congress.gov, bill, housebill.
31. H.R. 771 Every Student Succeeds Act, 116th Congress, 20192010, accessed April 17, 2020, Congress.gov, bill, housebill.
32. "National Education Technology," US Department of Education Releases, accessed January 19, 2019, https://www2ed.gov/about/lading.jhtml.
33. Anne Meyer, David H. Rose, and David Gordon, *Universal Design for Learning: Theory and Practice*, Wakefield, MA: CAST Professional Publications Online, accessed October 15, 2020, https://www.cast.org/our-work/publications/2014/universal-design-learning-theory-practice-udl-meyer.html#.XpixFZl7k2w.
34. "Universal Design for Learning," Principle I, Guideline 1, Checkpoint 1.1,14. CAST, accessed March 15, 2020, https://www.udlguidelines.cast.org.
35. "Universal Design for Learning," Principle II, Guideline 4, Checkpoint 4.1,22. CAST, accessed March 15, 2020, https://www.udlguidelines.cast.org.
36. "Universal Design for Learning," Principle III, Guideline 7, Checkpoint 7.1, 28. CAST, accessed March 15, 2020, https://www.udlguidelines.cast.org.
37. Maria Montessori, *Maria Montessori: The Secret of Childhood* (New York: Ballantine Books, 1979), 122.
38. Montessori, *Maria Montessori*, 122.
39. Individuals with Disabilities Education Act, Sec. 300.114 LRE requirements, accessed January 5, 2020, https://sites.ed.gov/idea/regs/b/b/300.114.
40. Jacqueline Cossentino, "Following All the Children: Early Intervention and Montessori. *Montessori Life* 2, no. 2 (2010): 1–8.
41. Individuals with Disabilities Education Act, Section 1414 (d) (3), accessed January 5, 2020, https://sites.ed.gov/idea/statute-chapter-33/subchapter-ii/1414/d/3.
42. Cossentino, "Following All the Children," 4.
43. McKenzie and Zascavage, "A Model for Inclusion," 32–38.

44. David Kahn, "The Deeper Meaning of Inclusion in Montessori Education," *NAMTA Journal* 39, no. 4 (2014): 11.
45. McKenzie and Zascavage, "A Model for Inclusion," 32–38.

BIBLIOGRAPHY

American Academy of Pediatrics Subcommittee on ADHD Disorder. *ADHD Clinical Practice Guidelines for the Diagnosis, Evaluation and Treatment of Attention Deficit Hyperactive Disorders in Children and Adolescents* 2011. Accessed January 25, 2020. https://pediatrics.aapublications.org/content/128/5/1007.

American Montessori Society. "About Montessori. Montessori for Children with Special Needs," Accessed April 2, 2020. https://www.amshq.org/about-Montessori/Montessori-for-children-with-special-needs-hasendorsementforspecialeducation.

American Montessori Society. *American Montessori Society Has Endorsement for Special Education*, 2019. Accessed June 2, 2019. http://www.amshq.org.

Boehnlein, Mary Maher. "The Montessori Research: A Review of Literature." *NAMTA Journal* 12, no. 1 (1987): 56–93.

CAST. *Universal Design for Learning Guidelines Version 2.0.* Wakefield, MA: Author, 2011. Accessed March 15, 2020. http://www.cast.org/our-work/about-udl.html.

CAST. *Universal Design for Learning Guidelines, Version 2.0*, 2014. Principle 1, Guideline 1, Checkpoint 1.1. Accessed March 15, 2020. http://www.cast.org/our-work/about-udl.html.

Cohen, David L. "Public Schools Embrace Montessori Movement." *Education Week* 9, no. 15 (1989): 1–14.

Cohen, David L. "Scientists' Panel Urges Big Boost in Child-Care Aid." *Education Week* 9 no. 26 (1990): 1–21.

Common Core State Standards: "Kindergarten Math Standards," 2019. Accessed November 3, 2019. https://www.ixl.com/printstandards/?statecc&stds.

Copple, Carol and Sue Bredekamp, eds. *Developmentally Appropriate Practice in Early Childhood Programs Serving Children from Birth through Age 8.* Washington, DC: National Association for the Education of Young Children, 2013.

Copple, Carol and Sue Bredekamp, eds. *Developmentally Appropriate Practice in Early Childhood Programs Serving Children from Birth through Age 8.* Washington, DC: National Association for the Education of Young Children, 2009.

Cossentino, Jacqueline. "Following All the Children: Early Intervention and Montessori." *Montessori Life* 2, no. 2 (2010): 1–8.

Danner, Natalie, and Susan Fowler. "Montessori and Non-Montessori Teacher's Attitudes toward Inclusion and Access." *Journal of Montessori Research* 1, no. 1 (2015): 29–41. Accessed January 26, 2020. https://digitalcommons,wou.edu/fac-pubs.

Deighton, Lee C., *Maria Montessori: The Encyclopedia of Education.* New York: Macmillan, 1971.

Elkind, David. "Piaget and Montessori." *Harvard Educational Review* 18, no. 2 (1967): 543.

Every Student Succeeds Act H.R. 771, 116th Congress, 2014-2015. Accessed April 17, 2020. https://www.ed.gov/essa.

Gitter, Lena L. *The Montessori Way.* Special Child Publication. Seattle, 1970.

Higher Education Opportunity Act H.R. 4137, 2007–2008. 2008. Accessed April 17, 2020. https://www2.ed.gov/policy/highered/leg/hea08/index.html.

Individuals with Disabilities Education Act, Sec. 300.114 LRE Requirements. Accessed January 5, 2020. https://sites.ed.gov/idea/regs/b/b/300.114.

Kahn, David. "The Deeper Meaning of Inclusion in Montessori Education." *NAMTA Journal* 39 no. 4 (2014): 1–11.

Kramer, Rita. *Maria Montessori Biography.* Chicago: University of Chicago Press, 1983.

Laski, Elida V., Jamilah R. Jor'dan, Carolyn Daoust, and Angela Murray. "What Makes Mathematics Manipulatives Effective? Lessons from Cognitive Science and Montessori Education." Sages and Open Access, 2015. Accessed March 4, 2018. http://www.uk.sagepub.com/aboutus/openaccess.htm.

Lillard, Angeline Stoll. *Montessori: The Science behind the Genius.* New York: Oxford University Press, 2005.

Lillard, Paula Polk. *Montessori: A Modern Approach.* New York: Schocken Books, 1972.

Matheson, Michael. "The First Montessori School in America." *America's First Impressions of Maria Montessori.* San Francisco: Fountainhead Montessori School, 1989.

Mastropieri, Margo A., and Thomas E. Scruggs. *The Inclusive Classroom: Strategies for Effective Differentiated Instruction.* Upper Saddle River, NJ: Pearson, 2018.

McKenzie, Ginger Kelley, and Victoria S. Zascavage. "A Model for Inclusion in Early Childhood Classrooms. *Montessori Life* 24, no. 1 (2012): 32–38.

Mercer, Cecil D., Ann. R. Mercer, and Paige C. Pullen. *Teaching Students with Learning Problems.* Boston: Pearson, 2011.

Meyer, Anne, David H. Rose, and David Gorden. *Universal Design for Learning: Theory and Practice*, 2014. Wakefield, MA: CAST Professional Publications. Accessed October 15, 2020. https://www.cast.org.

"Montessori Census," Montessori Census. Accessed March 25, 2020. https://www.montessoricensus.org.

Montessori, Maria. *Maria Montessori: The Secret of Childhood.* New York: Ballantine Books, 1979.

Montessori, Maria. *The Absorbent Mind.* New York: Dell Publishing, 1989.

National Association for the Education of Young Children. "About NAEYC," 2011. Accessed June 14, 2018. https://naeyc.org/content/about-naeyc.

National Association for the Education of Young Children. "About NAEYC Membership," Accessed June 14, 2018. https://naeyc.org/content/about-naeyc.

National Association for the Education of Young Children. "About NAEYC Membership," 2011. Accessed November 14, 2019. https://www.naeyc.org/membership.

National Association for the Education of Young Children. *Early Childhood Mathematics: Promoting Good Beginnings*, 2002, 2010. Last modified 2010. https://www.NAEYC.org/files/NAEYC/file/positions/psmath.

National Association for the Education of Young Children. "NAEYC Standards for Early Childhood Professional Preparation," 2009. Accessed October 2, 2018. https://www.naeyc.org/sites/default/files/globally_shared/downloads/PDF/resources.

National Autistic Society, "Obsessions Repetitive Behavior and Routines," 2016 Accessed October 2, 2018. http://www.autisium,org,uk.

National Center for Montessori in the Public Sector. "Number of Montessori Teacher Education Programs." Accessed June 2, 2019. https://www.public-Montessori.org.

National Center for Montessori in the Public Sector. "Inclusion Momentum in Montessori A.M.S. Accredited Programs." Accessed June 2, 2019. https://www.public-Montessori.org.

National Council of Teachers of Mathematics. *Principles and Standards for School Mathematics.* Accessed January 5, 2018. https://www.nctm.org/standards-and-positions/principles-and-standards.

"National Education Technology," U.S. Department of Education Releases. Accessed January 19, 2019. https://www.2ed.gov/about/lading.jhtm/.

North American Montessori Teacher Association. Accessed September 28, 2019. http://www.montessori-namta.org.

"Number of Montessori Teacher Education Programs." Montessori Census. Accessed March 25, 2020. https://www.montessoricensus.org.

Orem, Reginald C., *Montessori and the Special Child.* New York: Capricorn Books, 2012.

Orem, Reginald C. (ed.). *Montessori: Her Method and the Movement: What You Need to Know.* New York: G. P. Putnam's Sons, 1974.

Pickering, Joyce S. "Montessori for Children with Learning Differences." *Montessori Life* 28 no. 2 (2017): 49–53.

Seldin, Tim, and Paul Epstein. *The Montessori Way.* Bradenton, FL: Montessori Foundation Press, 2003.

Standing, Edwin M. *The Montessori Revolution in Education.* New York: Schocken Books, 1966.

US Department of Education Releases National Education Technology Plan 2916. Accessed January 10, 2020. https://www.2.ed.gov/about/landing.jhtml.

Chapter Two

Practical Life

The Montessori Early Childhood Inclusive Classroom: Creating a Cherished Experience

My Le N. Vo

Dr. Maria Montessori started her amazing career taking care of children with challenges when she was appointed assistant doctor at the Psychiatric Clinic in the University of Rome. She studied the works of two French doctors who took care of children with special needs: Jean Itard and Edouard Seguin.

Painstakingly, she translated the pioneers' work into Italian in order to thoroughly understand their thoughts. Equipped with thorough research and meticulous, careful observation of children with challenges (and later, children without challenges), Dr. Montessori created an outstanding method of teaching that has immensely benefited the educational international community.

In this chapter, the Montessori Practical Life learning experiences and lessons are connected to the National Association of the Education of Young Children (NAEYC) Standards and the Universal Design for Learning (UDL) Guidelines where appropriate. References for these connections can be found in the endnotes of this chapter.

The behaviors and responses of students and teachers to Montessori Practical Life methods described in this chapter are those observed in Montessori classrooms in Texas or related by Montessori Early Childhood teachers in Texas.

DR. MONTESSORI'S PEDAGOGICAL PRINCIPLES AND NAEYC INFORMATION

More than one hundred years after Montessori created it, the principles in the Montessori method are still strong and valid and continue to amaze educators with their thoroughness. The teachers follow and efficiently guide all students—both those with and without challenges—toward remarkable academic achievement.

What are those essential principles? It is beneficial for educators to re-analyze Dr. Montessori's thoughts in order to deepen awareness and assess the impact of Practical Life activities on the growth of young learners.

The NAEYC Standard 1 requires that teachers "use their understanding of young children's characteristics and needs and of the multiple interacting influences on children's development and learning to create environments that are healthy, respectful, supportive, and challenging for each child."[1]

The Prepared Environment

Dr. Montessori advised educators to prepare an environment filled with beauty as well as pleasant, age-appropriate activities through which the child can interact with his or her surroundings most productively. Dr. Montessori said,

> Just as the physical embryo needs its mother's womb in which to grow, so the spiritual embryo needs to be protected by an external environment that is warm with love and rich in nourishment, where everything is disposed to welcome, and nothing to harm it."[2]

In a stimulating prepared environment, Montessori teachers display concrete learning materials, each of which contains an abstract concept. After the teacher carefully presents the concrete material to the student, the teacher encourages each child to manipulate it. Dr. Montessori explained, "We know that it is through activity that development takes place."[3]

As a child works with the material repeatedly, he or she will gradually understand the abstract concept. Encouraging learning that develops from the hand to the mind, from holding something in the hand to holding a concept in the mind, is a valuable teaching principle.

Montessori educators know that repetition helps to ensure thorough understanding and mastery. According to Dr. Montessori, young children enjoy repeating their work. Montessori said, "The children were filled with life and resembled those who have experienced some great joy."[4] It is said that practice makes perfect. Indeed repetition assists the work of the cerebellum, "a mass of nerve cells that is the largest part of the human brain."[5]

Montessori teachers give their students activities that allow synthetic movement, movement that harmoniously combines mind and body. Young learners are invited to participate in activities that are directed by the mind toward intelligent purposes. As an example, in the plant-watering work, the child's mind directs all body movements, step by step, toward caring for a plant.

Dr. Montessori also advised educators always to proceed from simple to complex, easy to hard, in order to help students feel safe and move confidently on the path of knowledge. She recommended use of the Three Period Lesson in presentations:

- **First Period: Presentation**   This is a square. This is a circle. This is a triangle.
- **Second Period: Recognition**   Show me the circle. Show me the square. Show me the triangle.
- Lift the square. Lift the triangle. Lift the circle.

Note: Second Period needs to be used the most in order to facilitate recognition.

- **Third Period: Testing Mastery**   What is this? What is this? What is this?

According to Dr. Montessori, it is essential to practice Analysis of Movement when presenting a lesson to children. To make lessons clear and precise, teachers need to break down an action into its component parts. That means to show step by step what needs to be done first, next, and last with a slow, deliberate movement. In Dr. Montessori's words, "the more carefully an exercise was taught in all its details, the more it became an object of endless repetition."[6] NAEYC[7] also emphasizes the importance of positive and careful interactions between the teacher and child.

WHAT ARE THE PURPOSES OF PRACTICAL LIFE LESSONS?

Dr. Montessori presented to young children real-life activities such as spooning, pouring, watering plants, and opening and closing items. Lofty goals are attached to each of those activities: The development of "Order, Concentration, Coordination, and Independence, also known as OCCI."[8] Much of the child's future academic achievement depends upon these qualities.

WHAT ARE THE AREAS OF PRACTICAL LIFE ACTIVITIES?

The areas of Practical Life Activities include: Ground Rules, Grace and Courtesy, Control of Movement, Care of the Environment, and Care of Self. Ground Rules need to be presented to the children at the start of the school year and re-presented daily. The teacher chooses one to three ground rules to present each day. The children participate in acting out each rule. Children enjoy participating and enthusiastically help their teachers.

Ground rules are important in establishing a safe, calm, respectful environment that promotes focus and concentration in young learners. According to Dr. Marlyn Appelbaum, "Children need to learn to live in the real world with its rules and limits."[9]

The Bell provides an example of a Ground Rule presentation. The teacher begins by explaining that she sometimes needs to share an important message with the students. To do so, she tells the students she will use the classroom bell. When the children hear the soft ringing of the bell, they need to stop, cross their arms, put their feet together, and listen to the teacher's message.

After delivering her message, the teacher will thank the children for listening and then invite some children to participate and reenact the bell presentation. The teacher acknowledges the children's correct actions and thanks the children for their help. The bell is a very respectful, positive way of communication between the classroom director and students with and without challenges. It ensures peace, respect, and calmness in the prepared environment.

In Grace and Courtesy, "Excuse Me" provides children an opportunity to practice manners. The teacher invites some children to sit in a circle and explains that whenever one needs to walk between two others, it's important to quietly say "Excuse me." The others will then make space so one can walk through. Several children are invited to take turns initiating the "Excuse me" exchange, ending by saying "Thank you" to the children who let them walk through. The teacher thanks the children for helping her teach the lesson on courtesy.

A child who needs additional support is first invited to watch two or three classmates model this activity. Then the teacher should invite the child who needs additional support to perform the procedure of walking between two friends, first saying "Excuse me" and then "Thank you."

"Bead Stringing" offers a beautiful example of Control of Movement, an area that contributes to strengthening the child's fingers, development necessary for holding a pencil. The teacher shows a child how to carry the basket of beads from the shelf to the work area by using two hands and holding the basket close to the body. The teacher places the basket quietly on the table and sits by the child's dominant side (i.e., on the right side, if the child is right-handed). Using pincer fingers (the thumb, index, and middle finger), the teacher picks up a bead, puts the string through it, and draws the bead along the string to the end knot. Next, the teacher invites the child to do the work.

When all the beads have been strung, she happily invites the child to wear the necklace or remove the beads and place the basket back carefully on the shelf. For a student needing additional support, fewer and larger beads may be put in the basket to allow for easier handling and faster completion. Upon completion, the child will have a necklace to wear proudly. Thus, in alignment with Principle II of the UDL,[10] the teacher provides alternatives in instructional materials, physical manipulatives, and technologies.

Another effective lesson in Control of Movement is Walking on the Line. The teacher demonstrates to a group of children how to walk on the line, a two-inch-wide colored tape placed on the floor of the classroom.

The teacher carefully walks along the line, touching her toes to her heels with each step, and invites one to three children to follow her. The teacher then invites other children to take turns walking on the line, acknowledging their focus in placing their heels close to their toes. The teacher may add music or ask children to hold a bell or a tray containing small objects from the environment (such as three cubes of the Pink Tower) to help them further develop their concentration, balance, and coordination.

The teacher also may offer additional encouragement and comfort to the student who needs additional support by walking next to the student. The teacher may invite the student with challenges to carry a light basket containing a piece fruit while walking on the line. This is an example of the UDL principle of optimizing individual choice to ensure the engagement of the student.[11]

In Care for the Environment, a fine example is Cloth Folding, an activity that strengthens eye-hand coordination and develops concentration. The child is invited to carefully unroll a rug, go find the cloth folding tray, and place it on the top left corner of the rug. The teacher takes the first square cloth, places it on the rug, and uses her index finger to trace the dotted horizontal line from left to right. The teacher then picks up the two top corners of the cloth and brings them down to touch its two bottom corners. The teacher carefully uses her palm to smooth the newly formed shape, a large rectangle.

The other remaining cloths are presented in the same careful procedure, tracing the dotted line or lines from left to right, top to bottom, and smoothing the newly formed shapes: a large triangle, a small square, and a small triangle. For a student who needs additional support, the Montessori guide invites the child to repeat the actions after the teacher presents each cloth shape. This provides offer additional hands-on participation and helps ensure focus.

In Care for the Environment, a favorite activity of students is Plant Watering. The teacher explains that the dry plant needs help. The teacher carefully puts on her apron and invites the child to do the same. At the top of the work table, moving from left to right, the teacher quietly places the dry potted plant with its saucer, the watering can, and the dish with a damp sponge.

The teacher then places the dry plant without the saucer inside the round basin in the middle of the table. The child is asked to go to the sink and fill the watering can to the line marked on its outside. The teacher demonstrates slowly pouring water into the pot, stopping when water comes out of the holes at the bottom of the pot. Lifting the pot with two hands, the teacher invites the children to watch the water draining into the basin.

The teacher asks the child to put the happy plant onto its saucer and to return it to its place on the window ledge. The teacher slowly empties the basin into the bucket under the table and then wipes each item. Next, the sponge is rinsed and squeezed dry, and all materials are put away. The water in the bucket may be poured onto a plant in the garden. The teacher praises the students for their focused attention in helping a plant. The happy plant can continue its job, making food for all parts of the plant to grow and releasing oxygen to purify the air everyone breathes.

To help a student who needs additional support, the teacher involves the child along the way, inviting the child to pour some water into the dry plant, to hold it while the water drains, and to help clean up. This gives an example of how the UDL[12] encourages educators and learners to work together for lessons to be successful.

In Care of Self, a favorite children's activity is Shoe Polishing. First, the teacher invites the child to wear an apron like hers. The teacher and the child carefully bring the shoe-polishing activity to the table. The teacher and the child unroll the mat and place each item in the order of use from left to right at the top of the mat, each on top of its own outline: brush, shoe polish container with sponge applicator, rubbing cloth, and damp sponge.

The teacher holds the brush in the right hand and removes dust from a shoe held firmly in the left hand. The teacher then asks a child to brush the other shoe. Next, the teacher picks up the shoe polish, removes the container lid, and places it back at the mat top. Then the teacher squeezes the bottle to get the sponge applicator wet and polishes a shoe, using a slow, circular motion. The teacher invites the child to do the same with the other shoe. Finally, the teacher picks up the rubbing cloth, and using a circular motion and going left to right, shines a shoe. The child then polishes the other shoe. The teacher praises the child for her or his focused attention and effort making the pair of shoes shine.

For a student who needs additional support, the Montessori guide invites the child to participate throughout the activity. The next time the student who needs additional support works with shoe polishing, he or she is paired with a calm and patient friend who helpfully guides the child to complete the work. As the UDL[13] affirms, effective presentation of an activity requires the presenter—whether a teacher or a friend—to use a calm and patient voice.

A TOUCH OF CULTURAL DIVERSITY

As classes are now composed of children of different nationalities, activity themes are included that interest a culturally diverse population. For instance, children can be invited to practice using chopsticks to transfer colorful items from one bowl to the next. Dolls of different skin colors are available for children to bathe and dress.

At the end of the year, children practice writing wishes in different languages and learn to say them correctly. An international end-of-year holiday card can feature student wishes written in different languages. Elementary and middle school students have opportunities to submit drawings depicting peace and love for inclusion in the card. Diverse and inclusive end-of-year celebration projects are often an annual student favorite.

HOW DO PRACTICAL LIFE ACTIVITIES BENEFIT CHILDREN IN AN INCLUSIVE CLASSROOM?

Since Practical Life activities involve the child's body and mind, these lessons are the synthetic movements Dr. Montessori urged teachers to use to help the children's total development. The NAEYC standards also include using appropriate early learning standards and resources to support the mind and body of the child.[14]

Learners in Montessori Early Childhood classes are encouraged each day to choose their favorite activities and to work with them carefully until completion. As JoAnn Deak notes, doing so helps stimulate the child's prefrontal cortex, "the part of the brain responsible for planning and making decisions."[15] Young learners are also encouraged to repeat their works projects in order to master them. This habit stimulates the work of the cerebellum, which controls "voluntary motor movements, perception, and more complex psychological processes."[16]

Teacher presentations of Practical Life lessons are carried out with care and enthusiasm. They also make use of movement analysis and the principle of simple-to-complex procedure presentation. Used together, these techniques develop students' love for work and for the environment.

Young children, both those with and without challenges, gradually become calmer, more orderly, more independent, and with lengthened attention span and strengthened concentration. Their eye-hand coordination is more fully developed. The benefits of Practical Life are evident in the joyful Montessori environment.

TEACHER OBSERVATIONS

Teachers enthusiastically share comments about benefits they have observed among students with challenges like mild autism, attention deficit disorder (ADD), and Asperger syndrome. Practical Life activities and synthetic movements in which mind and body work together help calm children and allow them to better follow directions and focus on tasks.

One day, a guest came to visit a student with challenges and was trying to find that child in the classroom. Finally, the teacher, Ms. Diaz, found the student completely focused on watering his plant in a corner of the room. Ms. Diaz shared with the guest that each morning she suggests the student with challenges make a choice between two activities. She added that she sometimes asks a calm and patient friend to work with the student.

Another teacher, Mr. Tyler, commented that it was thanks to Practical Life activities that a student with attention deficit hyperactive disorder (ADHD) gradually was able to slow down and complete work. It was as if the student became a new child—calmer, more comfortable, happier, and more focused. The student's contentment was visible as she used her two fingers to trace the dotted line on the cloth and slowly folded it, or as she patiently swept all the dry beans into the square and used the dustpan to carefully gather them.

Another teacher, Ms. Cohen, described how content a student challenged by Asperger syndrome appeared while he concentrated fully on his sewing project. The student also became more focused in the other activities in the classroom.

UDL states that it is very important to provide information in a format that allows the child a new avenue to learning through the use of many different physical models or materials.[17]

The steady, continuous acquisition of order, concentration, coordination, and independence helps develop confidence and enjoyment of learning in all young learners—those with and without challenges. It ensures students' success in future academic endeavors.

Teachers feel privileged to have the opportunity to observe this development as the students as grow up. From the toddler program through early childhood and continuing to the end of middle school, teachers are excited to witness the positive results of the enlightening Montessori Method of education.

A DEEPENED AWARENESS

Daily observations and written-journal responses of students, including those who needed additional support, led teachers to identify five areas of growth: emotional, physical, social, academic, and spiritual. Practical Life activities fulfill young learners' strong need for order. The exercises are on the shelves, in their designated places, inviting learners to choose from them and carry out the task. The next day and in succeeding weeks, the activity can be repeated as wanted.

Such procedures help boost young learners' self-confidence, self-esteem, and independence. As children, including those who need additional support, actively work with Practical Life lessons, gross and fine-motor skills are strengthened, and balance and coordination are enhanced. Educators understand that developed eye-hand coordination is essential in future reading and writing activities. NAEYC Standard 3 states that practicing careful assessment of each child, including those with and without challenges, promotes positive outcomes.[18]

Following the teacher's directions and acting out daily ground rules along with grace and courtesy exercises allows the young child to gradually internalize important values. Acquisition of respect for self, others, and the environment contributes to future harmonious adaptation to living in society.

As the child, including the student who needs additional support, observes the teacher's careful presentations of lessons and subsequently works each lesson to completion, he or she develops a deepening joy of learning. Any activity that is started needs to be completed, with materials brought back to the shelf clean and ready for the next worker.

Young learners thus gradually acquire good work habits, inner discipline, and a growing sense of responsibility—important factors in the development of spiritual strength. The NAEYC Standard 4 states that the child should have positive outcomes as a result of classroom experiences.[19]

STRENGTHENED PERSPECTIVES

The opportunity to review the essential principles of Dr. Montessori's thoughts and to analyze the benefits of Practical Life activities in the development of normal and challenged young learners was a truly remarkable experience. It renewed the teachers' faith in Dr. Montessori's teachings, deepened their gratitude for the contributions of talented pioneers in education, and strengthened their perspectives on teaching methods.

Carefully preparing the child's environment, using age-appropriate materials to encourage repetition, teaching from simple to complex, and practicing analysis of movement in lesson presentations enabled teachers to rediscover the time-proven logic and thoroughness of Dr. Montessori's philosophy.

The teachers rejoiced in witnessing the resulting positive impact on students in all the five areas of development: physical, emotional, social, academic, and spiritual. The teachers noticed that, while challenged students need additional time for repetition, they—like their peers—profit in positive development. The students also need the warm encouragement of teachers.

As the UDL clearly states, "One of the most important things a teacher can do is to create a safe space for learners."[20] Dr. Pierre Faure, a renowned early childhood French educator once said, "A child is not a vase to be filled, but a source of possibilities."

As teachers create a cherished experience for students through using the very best practices of the Montessori Method, they can be confident that the students are developing into capable, responsible, respectful students. Each child, in his or her own way, is on the path to becoming a masterpiece.

NOTES

1. NAEYC, *NAEYC Standards for Early Childhood Professional Preparation: Position Statement Approved by the NAEYC Governing Board July 2009*, accessed October 2, 2018, Standard 1, key element 1c, 11, https://www.naeyc.org/sites/default/files/globally-shared/downloads/PDF/resource.

2. Maria Montessori, *The Secret of Childhood.* (New York: Ballantine Books, 1972), 34.

3. Maria Montessori, *The Absorbent Mind.* (New York: Dell Publishing, 1989). 80.

4. Montessori, *The Secret of Childhood*, 120.

5. Thomas J. Berndt, *Child Development* (Madison, WI: Brown and Benchmark, 1997), 172.

6. Montessori, *The Secret of Childhood*, 120.

7. NAEYC, *NAEYC Standards for Early Childhood Professional Preparation: Position Statement Approved by the NAEYC Governing Board July 2009*, accessed October 2, 2018, Standard 4, key element 4a, 14, https://www.naeyc.org/sites/default/files/globally-shared/downloads/PDF/resource.

8. Marlyn Appelbaum, *Practical Life Manual* (Houston: Marlyn Appelbaum, 1980), 1.

9. Ibid.

10. CAST. *Universal Design for Learning Guidelines Version 2.0* (Wakefield, MA: Author, 2011). Principle II, Guideline 4, Checkpoint 4.1, 22.

11. Ibid., Principle III, Guideline 7, Checkpoint 7.1, 28.

12. Ibid., Principle I, Guideline 1, Checkpoint 1.1, 14.

13. Ibid., Principle I, Guideline 1, Checkpoint 12, 15.

14. NAEYC, *NAEYC Standards for Early Childhood*, Standard 5, key element 5c, 16.

15. JoAnn Deak, *Your Fantastic Brain.* (New York: Scholastic, 2013), 8.

16. Berndt, *Child Development*, 172.

17. CAST. *Universal Design for Learning*, Principle I, Guideline 1, Checkpoint 1.3, 15.

18. NAEYC, *NAEYC Standards for Early Childhood*, Standard 3, key element 3.c., 13.

19. Ibid., Standard 4, key element 4.d, 14.

20. CAST. *Universal Design for*, Principle III, Guideline 7, Checkpoint 7.3, 29.

BIBLIOGRAPHY

Appelbaum, Marlyn. *Practical Life Manual.* Houston: Marlyn Appelbaum, 1980.

Berndt, Thomas J. *Child Development.* Madison, WI: Brown and Benchmark, 1997.

CAST. *Universal Design for Learning Guidelines Version 2.0.* Wakefield, MA: Author, 2011.

Deak, JoAnn. *Your Fantastic Elastic Brain.* New York: Scholastic, 2013.

National Association for the Education of Young Children. *NAEYC Standards for Early Childhood Professional Preparation: Position Statement Approved by the NAEYC Governing Board July 2009.* Accessed October 2, 2018. https://www.naeyc.org/sites/default/files/globally-shared/downloads/PDF/resource.

Montessori, Maria. *The Absorbent Mind.* New York: Dell Publishing, 1989.

Montessori, Maria. *The Secret of Childhood.* New York: Ballantine Books, 1972.

Chapter Three

Montessori Sensorial

The Montessori Early Childhood Inclusive Classroom: Creating a Cherished Experience

Crystal Dahlmeier

The Sensorial Curriculum in a Montessori classroom is unique and has been developed with specific aims to support children's development. This chapter describes those aims, outlines the specific qualities of the materials, and provides examples of the materials and ways that they can be adapted to meet the needs of both typically developing children and children who need additional support.

In this chapter, the Montessori Sensorial learning experiences and lessons are connected to the National Association for the Education of Young Children (NAEYC) Standards and The Universal Design for Learning (UDL) Guidelines where appropriate. References for these connections can be found in the endnotes of this chapter.

KEYS TO THE INTELLECT

"The aim is not an external one."[1]

Example 1: Mary (not her real name) is a 4.5-year-old girl who has been diagnosed with autism. She attends a Montessori preschool one day a week. She does not have expressive language at this time. Her experiences with the Montessori sensorial material are quite different from typical experiences. Occasionally, she demonstrates that she is learning classroom procedures by getting a rug on which to put her work, but she is not consistent.

Sometimes she carries the two longest red rods around the environment with her while she looks at what others are doing. Sometimes a teacher will get a rug out for her, and Mary will get the two thinnest brown prisms. She will hold them while the teacher places the remaining brown prisms on the rug.

When all ten are on the rug, often Mary will put them in sequence. Sometimes she guides the adult's hands to the one she wants placed next in the sequence. Often she walks away before the work is returned to the shelf, but sometimes she waits so she can place the two thinnest ones back on the shelf.

Mary is learning about the classroom routines and visual/tactile concepts of dimension in a way that works for her, without any harm to the materials or interfering with the work of other children.

Maria Montessori developed a sensorial curriculum that she considered both scientific and mathematical.[2] Montessori believed that it is through the sensorial experiences that the mind is able to identify, classify, seriate and sequence information, form judgments, and make comparisons. These qualities are recognized today as important aspects of executive function. The materials provide strong sensory stimulation and are often multisensory in order to accommodate a wide range of learning styles and abilities.

The NAEYC recommends that educational practices build on children's experience and knowledge, using their individual approaches to learning and their informal knowledge.[3]

Montessori identified the sensorial curriculum as the keys to the intellect.

SENSITIVE PERIOD FOR SENSATION

A sensitive period can be defined as a specific and limited time period when an individual is more attuned to a particular aspect of the environment to which they are biologically programmed to respond. According to Montessori, "these are of such intense activity that the adult can never recapture them, or recollect what they were like."[4]

According to the NAEYC Standard 4, the child's "natural interest and disposition to make sense of the world is where the engaged child uses touch, feeling, and the movement of materials to explore, classify, and make sense of the physical world."[5]

Montessori identified a sensitive period for refinement of the senses during the early childhood period. "The senses, being explorers of the world, open the way to knowledge. Our apparatus for educating the senses offers the child a key or guide to his explorations of the world."[6]

QUALITIES OF THE LESSONS

The lessons given by the guide are brief and practical and begin with concrete materials that the child can explore sensorially. The introductory lesson that the teacher gives demonstrates a way that the child can successfully interact with the material. The teacher names the material. "This is the Pink Tower and it is done on a work rug." With the child, the teacher demonstrates each step of the process, from retrieving and unrolling a work rug to carrying the cubes of the tower one at a time to the rug.

Depending on the child's interest and attention, the teacher can complete a full presentation from beginning to end or she can engage the child in the process. Following the presentation, the child is free to work with the material, repeat the presentation, and explore various ways to build the tower.

Through each hands-on experience, the child is both mentally and physically engaged, working independently and developing increasing concentration, order, and coordination. Cognitively, the child is experiencing (visually and through touch) a mathematically graded series. The Pink Tower is a perfect example of how Montessori lessons fit into the NAEYC education standards, in particular the Standard 7, which states the child will learn to "integrate mathematics with other activities and other activities with mathematics."[7]

THE GUIDE

Example2: Joseph, a four-year-old, is easily distracted. He plays with the activities on the shelf but runs away when the teacher encourages him to get a rug to do the work. He goes back to two or three materials regularly, especially the cylinder blocks, the geometric solids, and snack. The teacher takes photos of those materials and has them in a special container for Joseph when he arrives.

The teacher shows the photos to Joseph and asks him which one he would like to do first. He selects the cylinder blocks. She takes him with her as she gets a rug, unrolls it, and walks with him to the shelf. She demonstrates how to carry the material to the rug, gives a brief, silent lesson (to focus his attention on the visual aspect of the material, and remains with him to show him how to return the work to the shelf and roll the rug.

After repeating this routine for several days, Joseph gets his photos when he arrives and selects the material that he wants to use first. The teacher plans to add photos of other materials as Joseph continues to develop his ability to make choices and follow the order and sequence of the materials presented.

The teacher in the classroom works with individual children or small groups. His or her role is to put the child in touch with the didactic materials that embody specific concepts. Indeed, Montessori identified these materials as "materialized abstractions"[8] since they were designed in such a way as to demonstrate concretely a specific concept or abstraction.

FROM CONCRETE TO ABSTRACT

The process of abstraction is individual, slow, and related to brain development and the child's experiences. There is a tendency for educators to try to hurry the process for external purposes. Also, because adults are so accustomed to functioning in the abstract, it is easy to think that if a child is able to repeat a fact that he or she has been told, then the information has been mastered abstractly. However, that is merely memorization; it does not further the child's learning and understanding.

Abstraction cannot be taught; it depends on the child's development, environmental experiences, and mental maturity. Immersing the child in sensorial experiences with materials that are concrete, ordered, sequenced, complete, and mathematically designed will provide the child with the time and the experiences to move from sensation to perception and eventually—in his or her own time frame—to conceptual understanding.

This stage of instruction aligns with the NAEYC Standard 2, which encourages teachers to build on children's experience and knowledge. This includes their cultural and community backgrounds, their approaches to learning, and their informal knowledge.[9] If the child is hurried through this stage, the child will attempt to memorize rather than understand, and future learning may be negatively impacted.

Only one new concept is taught at a time. This "isolation of the difficulty" helps the child focus attention on the primary concept to be learned. With the Pink Tower, the mathematical concept is volume. The cubes vary in a mathematically precise sequence from one cubic centimeter to ten cubic centimeters. All ten cubes are identical except for the volume dimension.

The ten-cube quantity supports the base-10 number system, and their arrangement as a tower makes their various volumes visually apparent, thus highlighting the purpose of the material and the mathematical concept. As the child carries each cube individually, from smallest to largest, the visual sense is reinforced by touch (size and weight).

All activities in this sensory area are purposeful, with specific educational aims that can be varied to respond to individual interests, developmental levels, and needs. This strategy decreases the distraction and threat of novelty.[10]

Direct aims for the sensorial materials are the education and refinement of the senses. Indirectly, each material supports the development of both math and language concepts. As described above, the mathematical concept inherent in the Pink Tower is discrimination of volume. The direct aim is the refinement of the visual sense of dimension, so that the child, through repetition, is able to see increasingly subtle differences. Language, when it is introduced, focuses on the terms *big* and *small* and the comparatives and superlatives.[11]

Montessori designed the materials to be self-correcting.[12] Whenever possible, a control of error is built into the activity. The control of error is an aspect of the material that shows the child, through her work, when an error has been made. In this way, the child can use problem-solving skills to try to correct the error on her own. This quality of the material encourages children to begin to monitor and evaluate their own work, leading to increasing independence as learners.

Self-correcting materials with a control of error help the child build skills in self-regulation. The child has the freedom to select the activity as often as she has interest. Through exploration and repetition of the activity, she gains additional insights and awareness of the process and develops confidence in her abilities.[13]

The Cylinder Blocks have a very clear control of error. They consist of four blocks, each containing ten cylinders with knobs, each cylinder fitting into its respective hole. If one cylinder is placed in the incorrect hole, another cylinder will remain that does not fit. The child realizes on her own that a mistake has been made, and she can then explore ways to correct the error so that all cylinders are correctly placed.

As the materials increase in difficulty, the control of error is less evident. For example, with the Pink Tower, if one cube is incorrectly placed, the tower most likely will not collapse, but the child will see the disharmony and will explore other ways the tower can be built.

One of the most difficult things a Montessori teacher must overcome is the tendency to correct children's cognitive errors. These errors, through repetition of the activity and increasing cognitive awareness, will most likely self-correct. In situations where the self-correction is not occurring due to developmental or cognitive issues, the educator, through observation and conferences with specialists and parents, will need to adapt the approach.

This is in keeping with the UDL principle of customizing the display of information as a tool to learning.[14] In designing or redesigning any lesson to meet the needs of an individual learner, it is important to heed Montessori's caution that the lesson must never exhaust or fatigue the child, but rather "should analyze all the steps necessary to teach in the most economical way."[15]

SEQUENTIAL LEARNING

In the education of the senses, a specific sequence is presented. This sequence builds on the developing cognitive and physical skills of the child. The first step is to isolate a sensation, highlighting that quality. Children arrive in Montessori early childhood programs having already experienced millions of sensory experiences. An example would be auditory development, in which children have heard a plethora of sounds: dogs barking, sirens, different and varied human voices, and so on. They recognize contrasts (a dog's bark sounds very different from a cat's meow).

In a Montessori environment, numerous activities are introduced that require identifying and matching similar sounds to refine those early sensory experiences. Finally, gradation is introduced. This requires auditory discrimination of sounds that have increasingly subtle differences. The sound cylinders demonstrate this aspect of the materials.

Sound Cylinders consist of two boxed sets of six wooden cylinders. When shaken, the cylinders of one set make sounds progressing from loud to soft. Each matches the cylinders of the second set. One set has blue caps and one set has red caps. The lid of each box corresponds in color to the caps on the cylinders.

A young child may experience one cylinder at a time, listening to the sound it makes when shaken, thus isolating one sound. An older child will be able to match the sound cylinders, by shaking one red one and then shaking the blue cylinders until a match is found. This introduction to a new material does not require regimented programming but a simplified initial presentation of the activity to children who are younger or have learning challenges.[16] All six pairs of cylinders can be matched, or the teacher may choose to isolate fewer pairs.

Additional auditory games can be played to refine auditory discrimination. The red cylinders can be taken to a table across the room; the child can be asked to shake one and then walk across the room to find the blue one that matches. This requires auditory memory.

An additional challenge would be to grade the cylinders by loudness. This requires only one set of six. The child's task is to arrange the cylinders from loudest to softest. Once again, the control of error is the child's auditory perception and acuteness of hearing. Keen observation by the teacher will help inform him of the child's auditory abilities to determine if additional activities and/or testing are necessary.

One game children enjoy requires the participation of six children. Each takes one of the sound cylinders. The task is for the children to arrange themselves in order by the loudness of the cylinder each is carrying, from the loudest cylinder to softest. Numerous other activities are possible with both the Sound Cylinders and the Montessori Bells, which introduce the concept of musical tone.

INTRODUCTION OF LANGUAGE

Example 3: Three-and-a-half-year-old Madeline does not speak at school. Her parents report that she speaks at home but not in other social settings. Madeline's teacher observed that Madeline often stands at the shelf where the color tablets are displayed. The teacher invites her to a presen-

tation of the first color box (matching primary colors) and shows her how to match the color tablets. The teacher uses no words, except to tell her the name of the activity and that she can do this work any time she likes.

Madeline does the work on her own every day for a week, carefully matching the colors on the tablets. The following week, the teacher invites Madeline and one of the older girls in the class to do the second color box (matching primary, secondary, and tertiary colors). During the work, the teacher engages the older child in conversation about the color names (to model language). She also asks Madeline to hand her specific colors, gauging Madeline's knowledge of color by her physical response rather than requiring a verbal answer.

The teacher encourages the two girls to continue to work together and observes that they repeat the work later in the week. At that time, they work together to look for other objects in the classroom that match each of the colors in the color box.

The young child is in a sensitive period for language development. This natural interest and sensitivity to language inherent in the young child enables him to make associations effectively and quickly between objects and the names of objects in his environment. Vocabulary is taught only after the initial sensory experience and is introduced using the Three Period Lesson, a technique developed by Edward Seguin, a French physician who worked with children with special needs in the 1800s.[17]

Before the Three Period Lesson, the child works with the materials and experiences the sensory stimuli without verbal interruption. Only after a period during which the child acquires sensory impressions does the teacher fix the idea or quality with a word in the presentation:

- First Period: Association of the sensory perception with the name. The adult says the word, using a simple sentence format and pointing to the correct object. Two or three contrasting objects are always presented at a time. "This is red." "This is blue."
- Second Period: Recognition of object corresponding to the name. This is identification and follows mastery of the first period. "Show me blue." "Show me red."
- Third Period: Remembering or recall of the name of the object. The child identifies the object and says its name: "This is red."

If the child makes an error during the lesson, the teacher goes back to the preceding period and reviews it without pointing out the error. It is possible that a child may remain in one period for several months before internalizing the language. Observation and options for individual choice are key components to accommodation.[18]

VARIATIONS AND EXTENSIONS

Example 4: Max is unable to walk due to trauma at birth. The teacher explains to the children that Max will need their help, both getting material and returning it to the shelf. She then takes Max on a tour of the classroom, showing him a variety of materials that are available. She also has photos of many of them and notices which materials Max seems to like. She will add those photos to a special container for Max, which will help if Max does not know the name of a material. During the morning, Max indicates which material he would like to use, and a child who is nearby is asked to retrieve the work for Max. Often, the child who gets the material will engage in the activity along with Max.

Frequently, lessons are presented in the form of games to arouse curiosity. Since all of the sensorial materials can be explored at a variety of cognitive levels, children with a wide range of interests are responsive to games. The general cycle of activity is as follows:

1. Presentation: The directress shows the child a way to work with the material that is simple and basic and highlights the purpose of the material.
2. Exploration: The child explores the materials and repeats the activity in his or her unique, personal way.
3. Language: To add a new point of interest, the directress introduces vocabulary using the Three Period Lesson format.
4. Games are introduced: With these extensions and variations, the child can explore and demonstrate his or her increasing understanding of the concepts.
5. Presentation of more complex aspects of the material: This additional information encourages more exploration.

The Geometric Solids provide a clear example of the cycle of activity. This material consists of three-dimensional wooden objects, all painted blue. The shapes are:

Cube	Cone	Sphere	Rectangular prism	Triangle-based pyramid
Cylinder	Ellipsoid	Ovoid	Triangular prism	Square-based pyramid

In addition, wooden bases for the solids are available.

- First Presentation: The teacher shows the child how to carry Geometric Solids (two or more) to the rug and feel the shapes of the solids.
- Exploration: Independently, the child takes the solids to the rug and sensorially explores the shape, finding that some roll, some stack, some are rounded, some have flat sides, and so on.
- Second Presentation: The teacher adds language by presenting vocabulary, using the Three Period Lesson format: "This is a cube." "This is a cone."
- Games are introduced: Some possible games include use of mystery bag; identifying what's missing, finding similarly shaped items in the classroom, making the shapes with clay, and so on.
- Presentation of more complex aspects: More aspects may include the introduction of the bases for the solids; comparison of two-dimensional and three-dimensional figures; and using paper, pencil, scissors, and tape to make a solid form from a flat piece of paper.

Because the Montessori Method advocates individualized learning and adapting lessons to the child, implementation of the Montessori curriculum can meet the NAEYC guidelines and the principles of UDL in environments that serve children with a wide range of learning differences and needs.

The Montessori Red Rods serve as a clear example. The Red Rods include ten rods, differing only in length. The shortest rod is ten centimeters long; the longest is one meter. Each rod increases in length by ten centimeters, the length of the shortest rod.

While the rods could be any color, it is essential that they all are the same color so that the only difference is in length. The difference in length is also uniform. Because each rod is ten centimeters longer than the next shortest rod, the eye is immediately drawn to the length.

There are ten rods, relating them mathematically to the base-10 number system. The children carry the rods individually to the workspace by holding each rod at both of its ends. This not only makes transport safer but also enables the child to feel how each rod increases in length. The length of the one-meter rod is quite a stretch for a young child and reinforces the multisensory aspect of the material.

In the first presentation, rods are placed in random order on the rug. The initial task is to arrange the rods in order, from longest to shortest. When a child is able to do this, language is introduced; first, by identifying the extremes—long and short—then by refining the language to include comparisons and superlatives.

A variety of games can be played to reinforce the concept or to adapt it to special needs:

- Using two work rugs with all rods on the first rug, the teacher takes one of the rods to the second rug. Then the teacher asks the child to go to the first rug and bring the next shorter or longer rod to the second rug. This continues until all rods have been taken to the second rug.
- Teacher and child take turns taking rods to the work rug.
- The child can use the rods to make a maze.
- The shortest rod can be placed next to the "nine" rod to show equivalencies. (This is a direct preparation for math.)
- Various combinations of rods can be explored. (This is an indirect preparation for addition.)
- If the child is unable to do so, the teacher or another child can carry all rods to the work area.
- The teacher can present fewer rods at a time to a child with challenges.

The Red Rods provide many different ways for a child to perceive and comprehend information about the dimension of length.[19] This is in keeping with the UDL principle of customizing the display of information as tool to learning.[20] The concrete and multisensory nature of the material invites children to explore the material in a variety of ways. From a basic introduction as outlined above, to opportunities to make one's own red rods with red ribbon or construction paper, or to write the words with descriptors, or to assign numbers to each of the rods, this material incorporates endless opportunities for learning at ever-deepening levels.

The child is also physically engaged in the process. Students are given "alternatives for rate, timing, speed, and range of motor action required to interact with the instructional materials."[21] The teacher can provide a variety of options to both engage the child's interest and support repetition and persistence.

Because children in Montessori environments are offered choices in the activities they choose—and responsibility for completing the work—they are developing self-regulation.[22] One important aspect of self-regulation is the personal knowledge each learner has of his or her own motivation, be it intrinsic or extrinsic.[23]

An Overview of the Sensorial Curriculum

The Sensorial curriculum area contains materials that support the education and refinement of all of the senses. They are placed on open shelves in sequential order. Most of the materials are multisensory, but they are arranged on the shelves according to the primary sense the material is designed to educate.

Visual materials are divided into three categories: dimension, color, and form. The dimensional materials (Pink Tower, Brown Stair, Red Rods, Knobbed and Knobless Cylinders) are designed to help the child refine her ability to visually discriminate increasingly subtle differences within each material. These materials can also be explored in combination.

Color tablets consist of three sets that are sequenced from simple matching of the primary colors, to matching of all the colors, and finally to grading a series of shades of colors.

Visual discrimination of form is extensive and composed of many materials. The Geometric Solids (described previously in this chapter) and the Geometric Cabinet introduce the child indirectly to geometry. The Geometric Cabinet consists of six drawers of plane geometric shapes.

Children trace the frames and insets, learn the names of the shapes, and then match them to three sets of cardboard cards that progress from the solid shape to simply an outline of the shape. Montessori reminds us that this is not analysis.[24] Instead, it is observation of form, an indirect preparation for the study of geometry in the child's experiences.

Other form materials include the Constructive Triangle boxes. This set of five flat, colored triangles encourages the child to experiment with a variety of triangles in order to make different plane figures.

The binomial and trinomial cubes, the final form materials, are concrete representations of the binomial and trinomial theorems. These have been designed as three-dimensional puzzles for the child to complete.

Materials for auditory development are the Sound Cylinders (described previously in this chapter) and the Musical Bells. Many of the auditory activities are designed to be interactive in small groups with the teacher. These include identifying high or low sounds and identifying environmental sounds or sounds in words.

In the tactile sense exercises, the child learns through her sense of touch. With the Baric Tablets, the child learns to feel the different weight of different objects. The Thermic Tablets emphasize the sense of temperature, and the Touch Boards and Fabric Matching help the child develop tactile sensitivity to a variety of surfaces.

In the Olfactory and Gustatory activities, the child discriminates between different tastes and smells. Many of these activities involve food preparation, snacking, or gardening.

Montessori identified the stereognostic sense or "muscular memory" that involves both vision and touch.[25]

SUMMARY

When people visit a Montessori environment, they are often impressed by the exquisite array of the sensorial learning materials. The colors, design, and placement of the materials attract both the eye and the hand. This appeal has been planned because the repeated use of the materials will assist the child in her passage from being a concrete learner to an abstract thinker. This passage is one that only the child can do for and by herself.

The child's interaction with the sensorial materials refines all the senses, leading to more accurate perception. It eventually prepares the learner for reading, writing, and mathematical activities. The journey is gradual; each step acquired in isolation gradually merges into understanding.

NOTES

1. Maria Montessori, *The Absorbent Mind* (New York: Dell Publishing, 1967), 186.
2. Ibid.
3. National Association of Young Children, *Developmentally Appropriate Practice in Early Childhood Programs Serving Children from Birth through Age 8*, position paper, 2009, 12. https://www.naeyc.org/sites/default/files/globally shared/downloads/PDFs/resources/position-statements/PSDAP.pdf.
4. Montessori, *Absorbent Mind*, 51.
5. National Association of Young Children, *Developmentally Appropriate Practice*, 14.
6. Montessori, *Absorbent Mind*, 182.
7. National Association of Young Children, *Developmentally Appropriate Practice*, 11.
8. Montessori, *Absorbent Mind*, 186.
9. National Association of Young Children, *Developmentally Appropriate Practice*, 12.
10. CAST, *Universal Design for Learning Guidelines Version 2.0.* (Wakefield, MA: Author, 2011), Principle III, Guideline 7, Checkpoint 7.3, 30.
11. Maria Montessori, *The Discovery of the Child* (Madras, India: Kalakshetra Publishing, 1966), 193.
12. Ibid., 140.
13. CAST, *Universal Design for Learning*, Principle III, Guideline 8, Checkpoint 8.1, 30.
14. Ibid., Principle I, Guideline 1, Checkpoint 1.1, 14.
15. Lena Gitter, *The Montessori Approach to Special Education* (Johnstown, PA: Mafex Association, 1971), 50
16. CAST, *Universal Design for Learning*, Principle III, Guideline 8, Checkpoint 8.2, 31.
17. Montessori, *The Discovery of the Child*, 193.
18. CAST. *Universal Design for Learning Guidelines*, Principle III, Guideline 7, Checkpoint 7.1, 28.
19. UDL Principle 1.
20. CAST, *Universal Design for Learning*, Principle I, Guideline, Checkpoint 1.1, 14.
21. Ibid., Principle III, Guideline, Checkpoint 4.1, 22.
22. Ibid., Principle III, Guideline 9, Checkpoint 9.1, 33.
23. Ibid.

24. Maria Montessori, *The Montessori Method* (New York: Schocken Books, 1964), 236.

25. Ibid., 188.

BIBLIOGRAPHY

CAST. *Universal Design for Learning Guidelines Version 2.0.* Wakefield, MA: Author, 2011. Accessed January 24, 2020. http://www.cast.org/our-work/about-udl.html.

Gitter, Lena L. *The Montessori Approach to Special Education,* Johnstown, PA: Mafex Association, 1971.

Montessori, Maria. *The Absorbent Mind.* New York: Dell Publishing, 1967.

Montessori, Maria. *The Discovery of the Child.* Madras, India: Kalakshetra Publishing, 1966.

Montessori, Maria. *The Montessori Method,* New York: Schocken Books, 1964

National Association for the Education of Young Children. *Developmentally Appropriate Practice in Early Childhood Programs Serving Children from Birth through Age 8*. Position Paper, 2009. Accessed October 2, 2018. https://www.naeyc.org/sites/default/files/globally-shared/downloads/PDFs/resources/position-statements/PSDAP.pdf.

Chapter Four

Early Childhood Montessori Mathematical Education

The Montessori Early Childhood Inclusive Classroom: Creating a Cherished Experience

Ginger Kelley McKenzie and Victoria S. Zascavage

Early childhood mathematical education in a Montessori setting is guided by the educational standards of the National Association for the Education of Young Children (NAEYC), Common Core Curriculum, and the tenets of the National Council of Teachers of Mathematics (NCTM). In a joint position paper, NAEYC and NCTM determined ten research-based interventions recommended for early childhood mathematics.[1]

These ten key recommendations provide structure within this chapter because in high-quality mathematics education for three- to six-year-old children, teachers, and other key professionals should:

1. enhance children's natural interest in mathematics and their disposition to use it to make sense of their physical and social worlds;
2. build on children's experience and knowledge, including their family, linguistic, cultural, and community backgrounds; their individual approaches to learning; and their informal knowledge;
3. base mathematics curriculum and teaching practices on knowledge of young children's cognitive, linguistic, physical, and social-emotional development.
4. use curriculum and teaching practices that strengthen children's problem-solving and reasoning processes as well as representing, communicating, and connecting mathematical ideas;
5. ensure that the curriculum is coherent and compatible with known relationships and sequence of important mathematical ideas;
6. provide for children's deep and sustained interaction with key mathematical ideas;

7. integrate mathematics with other activities and other activities with mathematics;
8. provide ample time, materials, and teacher support for children to engage in play, and provide a context in which they explore and manipulate mathematical ideas with keen interest;
9. actively introduce mathematical concepts, methods, and language through a range of appropriate experiences and teaching strategies; and
10. support children's learning by thoughtfully and continually assessing all children's mathematical knowledge, skills, and strategies.[2]

This chapter blends NAEYC recommendations with Universal Design for Learning (UDL), State Common Core Standards, and Montessori educational pedagogy. When appropriate, references for these connections can be found in the endnotes of this chapter. Because this chapter addresses a variety of challenges some Montessori classroom students face in early childhood mathematics, it will use the expression "students who need additional support" rather than the more restrictive one, "children with disabilities." At this early age, learning difficulties may have many possible explanations, such as developmental delays, lack of appropriate instruction, or diagnosed disability.

Within the Montessori program, preparation of the classroom promotes instructional regulation and creates an opportunity for routine, both of which lead to independence. Classroom preparation also provides support for all children to learn as they become familiar with the materials for math and geometry, which naturally embraces the lessons learned in Practical Life and Sensorial. For the student who needs additional support to assist with attention deficit disorder (ADD), autism, or developmental delay, this chapter describes strategies and materials common to the Montessori classroom and correlated with the principles of UDL.

While most children are not checked for attention deficit hyperactivity disorder (ADHD) until they are school age, they can be diagnosed as early as age 4, according to guidelines set by the American Academy of Pediatrics (AAP).[3] The strategies described here promote the acquisition of practical mathematical skills as well as basic number and operations concepts. These concepts are designed to assist all children, including those with ADD, autism spectrum disorders, and developmental delays.

In the Montessori classroom, the Prepared Environment is a critical component of early mathematical learning. The environment in the Montessori classroom is prepared to allow for the child to absorb knowledge by immersion in a progression of mathematical activities that follows a specific order, building from simple to complex. The child is placed in a setting that allows freedom to explore within the Prepared Environment.[4]

The aim of the Prepared Environment, initially presented in the Practical Life lessons, is to create independence, a sense of ownership of the task at hand, and an overall growing sense of self-efficacy. In this spirit, the child, after the initial Long Rods Presentation in the Sensorial curriculum, is encouraged to revisit this activity. This opportunity supports the independent learning experience. The teacher quietly keeps watch for obstacles that may intrude on the child's ability to become an independent learner.

Example 1: Ms. Laura, a Montessori teacher, is observing 4-year-old Ella, who has been diagnosed with ADHD, to whom Ms. Laura has presented the Long Rods 1, 2, and 3. Ms. Laura asks Sally, a five-year-old, to re-present the Long Rods 1, 2, and 3 to Ella, letting Ella carry each rod from the sensorial shelf to the work rug. Ella has lots of energy and enjoys carrying each long rod to the work rug. After Sally re-presents the Long Rods, it is exciting to see Ella choose this same work later in the day. Ella independently does the work and carefully returns the materials to the sensorial shelf.

Maria Montessori encouraged the concept of exploration to engage the curiosity of all children, including those children who need additional support. This concept still has merit in the twenty-first century concept of special education. Students with certain exceptionalities may need a more structured introduction to engage in the exploration of the Prepared Environment. This introduction does not require scripted or regimented programming but rather a simplified initial presentation of the activity. For example, when beginning the Geometric Cabinet, the Presentation Tray of the Geometric Cabinet would not be shown to the student who needs additional support. This accommodation is a differentiation based on degree of difficulty and complexity.[5]

The Prepared Environment helps guide the immature learner and the student who needs additional support to find calm, order, and safety in the learning activity. Order in the environment creates predictability and safety in repetition and does not waste intellectual or physical energy. Preparing the mathematical environment in an inclusive classroom where everything has a designated space creates a sense of security; change can be a true stumbling block for those children on the autism spectrum who thrive in a situation with predictable routines as a means of coping with everyday life.[6] This strategy decreases the distraction and threat of novelty.[7] As Montessori has stated, "The children, properly guided, of course, actually enjoy preserving this order which they find around them."[8]

According to NAEYC Standard 1, "To achieve high-quality mathematics education for 3- to 6-year-old children, teachers and other key professionals should enhance children's natural interest in mathematics and disposition to use it make sense of their physical and social worlds."[9] Montessori refers to this as the "sensitive period," when a child is motivated to acquire this knowledge.[10] NAEYC Standard 4 refers to this process as "strengthening children's problem solving and reasoning processes as well as representing, communicating, and connecting mathematical ideas."[11]

Interest in mathematical relationships begins in the Practical Life area where children manipulate materials to emulate adult activities (pouring, transferring materials from one container to another, sorting, and classifying) that lead to the preparation of their own snacks. Sequencing and classifying activities, such as learning how to prepare toast, serve the snack to a friend, and put the snack materials away, are part of the standard Montessori curriculum in Practical Life.

Example 2: The snack table in Ms. Laura's 3–6 classroom is an important part of the environment and snack time provides a predictable routine each day. Many times it also incorporates practical math lessons. Timmy, a four-year-old second-year learner, is paired with Lacy, a new four-year-old child who has had an early diagnosis of autism. Each day, Timmy reads Lacy the card about the snacks for the day. Ms. Laura provides snacks that require counting out what each child puts on his or her small glass plate. (Example: four grapes and two wheat crackers). After each snack, the children carefully clean up their own dishes. This routine is repeated daily. This repetition is very important to the success of children with autism, such as Lacy.

The snack-time routine in the Montessori classroom builds on the children's family experience and community background, their linguistic and cultural knowledge, their individual approaches to learning, and their informal knowledge. It also relates their knowledge to the vocabulary and conceptual frameworks of mathematics. In other words, it "mathematizes" what they intuitively grasp.[12]

PRACTICAL LIFE AND THE POURING ACTIVITY

Young children begin their mathematical education in the areas of Practical Life when they engage in a sequential Pouring Activity. The young child learns to pour rice from a bigger container into several smaller containers. This Pouring Activity allows for the exploration of the Newtonian principle of conservation of mass and the initial introduction of the geometric concept of volume. If a child does not correctly carry out the Pouring Activity, the entire sequence is modeled again by the teacher.

For the child with a developmental delay or others who have not demonstrated the ability to initiate the sequence, picture prompts facilitate independence by assisting short-term memory. This accommodation helps the child to build skills in self-regulation by supporting the ability to remember and maintain the initial goal.[13] The picture prompts should be phased out gradually as the child demonstrates they can do the activity without these prompts. The use of picture prompts is also suggested for young children on the autism spectrum if they respond positively to picture-based visual prompts. Picture cards are two sided. On one side is a photograph of the step to take (e.g., a child pouring water into a container). The other side has the summative word "pour."

Montessori is designed to move away from scripted lessons. As the child becomes more confident with an activity, picture prompts should be phased out.[14] Please note that in the spirit of UDL, in which classroom activities are intended for the participation of all children, the Pouring Activity can be conducted with rice, dry oatmeal, cornmeal, or water. This is in keeping with the UDL principle of customizing the display of information as a tool to learning.[15]

Example 3: In Ms. Laura's classroom, once a child has accomplished the task of pouring water, this activity is added to the daily snack-table preparation. The child is given a choice of water or juice. After the new 4-year-old Lacy learns to pour, she is ready to add water or juice to her snack each day. Interestingly, the day Lacy learns to pour her own water, she asks for the lessons on how to arrange flowers for the snack table. This is a great example of an extension of Practical Life experiences available to the children every day.

SENSORIAL PREPARATION AND DIMENSIONAL ACTIVITIES

Dimensional Activities are lessons about the geometric properties of length, width, height, and thickness. These lessons are introduced along with the appropriate vocabulary in the early childhood classroom. Examples of these activities are the Broad Stair Lesson, the Pink Tower Lesson, and the Long Rod Lesson. The Broad Stair Lesson introduces the concept of thick and thin. The ten wooden prisms are twenty centimeters long and range in thickness from one to ten centimeters. The Broad Stair prisms, when stacked from the thickest to the thinnest, create a staircase that can be flat on the floor or stacked on top of each other to make a tower. The word "prism" is introduced during these dimensional activities.

The Pink Tower Lesson introduces the word "cube" and the concept of big and small. The ten pink cubes range in size from a one-centimeter base to a ten-centimeter base.[16] This is an example of how Montessori classrooms introduce knowledge of the metric system.

Example 4: Ms. Laura moves one cube at a time, starting with the smallest cube. Rather than being introduced to ten cubes, a student needing additional support will only be introduced to three cubes (preselected to be the first cube, third cube, and fifth cube), which are placed on the mat side by side.

The Long Rod Lesson uses Red Rods that are uniform in cross-section but vary in length from ten centimeters to one meter long. The teacher models the Long Rod Exercise first, and then the child holds each rod with two hands, carries them one by one to the mat, and places each rod anywhere on the work surface. The Red Rod Activity presents a progression of length that simulates the natural progression of the numbers one to ten. Throughout the activity, the vocabulary of length (longest, shortest) is used.

For some students who need additional support, the number of trips required to transport the materials needed for the three Sensorial Activities might be overwhelming. To promote the pleasurable aspect of sensorial and/or mathematical exploration, it is advisable to gauge factors that precipitate frustration. Children with developmental delays, autism, and ADD might need ten trips to transport the long rods in the correct manner to avoid a sensory overload or to provide much-needed kinesthetic relief. Observation and providing options for individual choice are key components to accommodation.[17]

Example 5: Ms. Laura is working with a child with autism who lost concentration and experienced sensory overload when carrying all ten long rods to the work rug. To accommodate the child's needs, Ms. Laura, asks the child to carry only three long rods, which is a good accommodation.

Because words are not the center of these spatial activities, children with language delay are not disrupted. NAEYC Standard 3[18] and the tenets of Montessori education[19] emphasize the importance of knowing the young child's levels of cognitive, linguistic, physical, and social-emotional development in order to allow for a natural progression of learning that guards against the risk of misclassifying individual children during these foundational activities of mathematics.

NUMBER ORDERING

The Sensorial and Practical Life Activities and Number Ordering are going on at the same time; they are not progressive or exclusionary. These three intertwine to allow the child to experience early number concepts in mathematics. The Montessori early childhood mathematical curriculum builds on known relationships and sequence. For example, once the child understands the concept of *one to ten* in the Number Activities, the teacher presents the Concrete Golden Bead material and the concepts of *unit*, *ten*, *hundred*, and *thousand*. One unit is one bead, a "ten bar" (which has ten beads on it) is called "ten," the "hundred square" (which has one hundred unit beads on it) is "one hundred," and the "thousand cube" (which has one thousand unit beads and ten "hundred squares") is one thousand.

Example 6: Ella, a 4-year-old child with ADHD, has worked with her classmate Sally on the number rods, so after her teacher, Ms. Laura, presents the concept of the unit, ten bar, and hundred square to Ella, Ms. Laura asks Sally to re-present the concepts to Ella.[20]

Montessori lessons are sequential, and as stated in NAEYC Standard 5, "ensure(s) that the curriculum is coherent and compatible with known relationships and sequences of important mathematical ideas."[21] Exploration and repetition develop dimensional relationships and early understanding of numbers. Self-selected activities are encouraged. The correct use of materials is emphasized, creating an expectation of creative but respectful use of all the materials. However, it should be carefully understood that exploration of materials is appropriate even when the intent of the activity is different from what the child is creating. The child should be guided into the correct procedures on another day. The first step in understanding numbers is the Counting Activity that uses the Number Rods and the Three Period Lesson format.[22]

THREE PERIOD LESSON FORMAT AND RELATIONSHIP TO DIRECT INSTRUCTION

Dr. Angeline Stoll Lillard, a developmental psychologist, suggests the Three Period Lesson format used by Montessori to teach and assess children learning mathematics "might be thought of as association, recognition, and recall."[23]

- First Period Lesson. The teacher clarifies vocabulary and shows the material to the child.
- Second Period Lesson. The teacher tests recognition by asking the child to show the correct material associated with the word: "Show me the One Rod."
- Third Period Lesson. When the child demonstrates recognition, the teacher assesses the child's understanding by asking, "What is this?"

Direct instruction is a research-based intervention for students with mild disabilities, autism, and ADD. The steps of direct instruction summarized from the University of Oregon model by Mercer and Pullen,[24] are similar to the Three Periods Lessons of Montessori,[25] and the standard components of direct instruction traditionally involve three steps:

- Step One: Specific objectives introduced in a structured lesson modeled and narrated by the teacher are followed by independent practice of concept as the teacher observes the child for correctness.

- Step Two: After independent practice by the student, the teacher asks specific factual content-related questions to check for concept mastery. For example, the teacher might point to a long rod the student just put out and ask, "Can you show me the one rod?" Re-teaching is conducted if the concept is not mastered.
- Step Three: The teacher makes a summative assessment of vocabulary by asking direct questions related to the concept.[26] The teacher asks, "What is this?"

In a Montessori classroom, if the teacher observes that the concept is not correctly performed or understood by the student, the teacher simply asks the child to put away the material and re-presents the material at another time. Maria Montessori determined that this stop-and-return methodology prevents the child from feeling defeated and curtails the practice/reinforcement of incorrect concepts.[27]

COUNTING: MONTESSORI METHODS OF INSTRUCTION

The NAEYC Standard 6 criteria for "children's deep and sustained interaction with key mathematical ideas"[28] in Montessori starts with the Number Rods. The Number Rods are similar to the Long Rods, but the first Number Rod is red and ten centimeters long, and each additional Number Rod changes length by adding ten centimeters, alternating in color from red to blue. Children develop a concrete understanding of the relationship of one to ten by associating wooden Numeral Cards (1, 2, 3, 4, 5, 6, 7, 8, 9, and 10) with wooden rods representing progressively longer lengths. Counting then progresses to the recognition of written symbols presented by the Sandpaper Numbers and Smooth Numeral Cards. This progression takes the child from concrete (rod) to abstraction (symbol) and can be a difficult concept to master for a child with challenges.

NUMBER ROD ACTIVITY

The Number Rod Activity addresses Common Core Standards for children ages 3 to 6 (K.CC.A.1) and 6 to 9 (K.CC.A.3). The standard refers to Kindergarten Counting and Cardinality—Count to tell the number of objects.[29] The purpose of the Number Rod Activity is to learn the names of the numeral (1–10) and associate the name with each Number Rod. Number sequencing leads to the ability to count using the Number Rods (concrete manipulative). This activity provides an introduction to the metric system as the longest Number Rod is one meter, and the shortest is ten centimeters. When given a set of ten red and blue rods, the child will place the rods in order by size from the shortest to longest rods. At the onset of this activity, the students who need additional support must be reintroduced to the sensorial concept of shortest to longest with the Number Rods, which are now painted red and blue.

Example 7: Since Timmy has helped Lacy, who has autism, with the Long Rods previously, it is consistent to ask him to show Lacy the 1, 2, 3 Number Rods this time and compare them to the 1, 2, 3 Long Rods. He can then continue to help Lacy with the 4, 5, 6 Number Rods.[30]

Any change in material for the student who needs additional support elicits the possibility of a generalization problem and must be dealt with before proceeding. The idea of generalization is to "extend the use of acquired skills across situations."[31] It is indeed a challenge and rarely happens spontaneously for the students who need additional support unless a detailed explanation of the new relationship to the mastered skill is provided. The materials from the early childhood classroom activities are used later with older Montessori children for the metric lessons in vocabulary and measuring items using meter and centimeter rods. This continuity of materials can decrease the anxiety of students on the autism spectrum who may be resistant to

First Period Lesson for Number Rods. The teacher models the lesson procedure by retrieving all the rods one at a time from the math shelf, starting with the One Rod. For the student with challenges, the teacher begins by bringing Number Rods One, Two, and Three only. The rods are placed on the child's mat or work surface. The teacher asks, "Can you find the shortest rod and place it on the lower part of the mat?" The teacher traces over the shortest rod saying, "This is one." The child traces the rod with his or her first two fingers and says, "One." The same procedure is followed for the Two Rod and the Three Rod. Each day, another number rod is added until all ten Number Rods are introduced.

Best practice is to vary the options for physical action according to the needs of the student providing "alternatives in the requirements for rate, timing, speed, and range of motor action required to interact with the instructional materials, physical manipulatives, and technologies."[32]

There is a standard way to carry the rods using one hand on the end of each rod. The method may need to be demonstrated using peer modeling or assistance. The goal is to move the rod safely from where it is stored on the math shelf to the mat. It may be necessary to have the rods available at the mat for children with physical limitations or processing difficulties.

Example 8. Ms. Laura asks Marcus to present Number Rods 1, 2, 3 to Tania, a 4-year-old child in a wheelchair. First, Marcus brings Number Rods 1, 2, 3 one at a time to Tania's work surface, a table with a rug she has placed on it.

Caution should be used to not introduce words such as "left-hand bottom corner" or "this half of the rug" when giving instructions to students who need additional support because this verbiage presents a dual relationship that may confuse the child. The child should be able to focus on the rod activity and not on description of placement. Teachers model the concept without extraneous vocabulary. The repetition and predictability of the first step can be beneficial for the child with autism who is comfortable with routine.

Second Period Lesson. When all ten numbers have been recognized by the child, the teacher assesses understanding by asking the child, "Show me the One Rod; show me the Two Rod." If the child responds correctly, the teacher continues up to the Ten Rod. When mastery of the rods *in sequence* has been demonstrated, the teacher asks for a Number Rod *out of sequence*.

For the student who needs additional support because of developmental delay or autism, it is important that the introduction to this Second Period Lesson be in the sequence of the first reiteration, which has only three rods ("Show me the One Rod. Show me the Two Rod. Show me the Three Rod.") This addition of the word "rod" keeps the concept concrete. When the child appears ready to move to the random challenge of the Second Period Lesson, it might be less confusing to present the challenge with three rods and slowly move up to the Ten Rod. Change can be traumatic for the student who needs additional support and often precipitates anxiety or outburst behavior as they may associate any change with their failure to adapt.

Third Period Lesson. The teacher makes a summative assessment by pointing to a single rod among the ten rods laid out in sequence and asks,

"What is this?" If the student does not answer with the correct numeral, the teacher will reintroduce the concept and return to the First or Second Period Lesson, depending on what the child's level of readiness.

SANDPAPER NUMERAL ACTIVITY

The Sandpaper Number Activity addresses the Common Core Standard KCC3:[33] "to represent a number of objects with a written numeral 0–20, with zero representing a count of no objects." The Montessori math curriculum begins with lessons that focus on the numbers one through nine. Experience with sandpaper letters in the language area and mastery of the Number Rods 1 to 10 are common prerequisites. The purpose of the Sandpaper Numeral Activity is to recognize the name of the numbers "1" to "9" and to put the numbers in counting order.

First Period Lesson. Teacher begins modeling the lesson by taking the sandpaper numeral one out of the box. The teacher places his or her left hand on the left side of the number and then traces over the sandpaper numeral one in the direction that it would be written while stating the name of the number. The number is handed to the student, who then repeats the procedure. The initial lesson begins with numbers one, two, and three. When this is mastered, the teacher reviews one, two, three, and introduces four. This progression continues until the numbers one through nine are mastered.

Children with autism may become overwhelmed with multiple sensory input using sandpaper numerals (i.e., the tactile sensation of tracing the sandpaper numeral, the visual representation of each numeral, and the auditory component of hearing the word). This sensitivity should have been previously identified with Sandpaper Letters in Language. Therefore, it may be necessary to use the Smooth Numeral Cards with the same procedure for any students who are sensory sensitive. Two other options for the child sensitive to rough items are to make a set of numerals out of felt or to use a set of magnet numerals for the child to trace.[34]

The First Period Lesson 1–9 should be mastered before moving onto the Second Period Lesson. Montessori activities offer a systematic approach and the flexibility to return to the activity as a cherished experienced.

There is a danger that the spatial shape is memorized without association with the concept of the number. Specifically, for the student who needs additional support and who is having difficulty mastering the concept of "1" through "3," there will follow many exercises to help the student with this association of the number of objects with the written numbers (i.e., Spindle Boxes, Mystery Game, Numerals and Counters).

Children with attention limitations should be presented with numerical groups of three at a time, first matching 1, 2, 3, then 4, 5, 6, and finally 7, 8, 9. The expectation is that the child will be able to do this activity independently.

To facilitate this event, it might be necessary for the young person with attention deficit to go and get each number, one at a time, from across the room. This physical movement provides kinesthetic relief. Three numbers will be in a specific box. After the three numbers are on the work surface, the student identifies the number "1" and claps one time. This movement "uses cues and prompts to draw attention to critical features."[35] This kinesthetic activity reinforces the value of the number and focuses attention.

It is important to note that the teacher cannot ask the students to select three given numbers (i.e., "Please get 4, 5, and 6.") as this is expecting an auditory processing, short-term memory, and attention rather than the skill of number recognition.

Second Period Lesson. The teacher asks the child to lay out the sandpaper numbers in order, and then asks the student to identify a specific number, for example, "Show me the three." For the student who needs additional support, a review starting with 1, 2, and 3 may be appropriate. Assess and then progressively add more numbers. Once the first three numbers are mastered, it may be reinforcing to have a peer modeling the entire exercise with the student who needs additional support.

Third Period Lesson. In the summative assessment of the Sandpaper Numbers Activity, the teacher makes two evaluations by asking the student 1) to lay out the numbers 1 to 9 in order and 2) to identify a number while the teacher points to it and asks "What is this number?" This question-and-answer assessment continues until the student can identify and pick up every number from 1 to 9. In order to foster the concept of generalization, the child then progresses to the one-to-one association of the smooth numeral cards with the corresponding sandpaper numeral cards. When this has been accomplished, the child, in order to foster generalization of concept, progresses to the one-to-one association of the smooth numeral cards with the sandpaper numeral cards. This activity is first modeled by the teacher and then performed by the child. For a student who is familiar with the smooth numeral cards but who may have autism and be uncomfortable touching rough items, a set of felt numeral cards or magnet numeral cards is suggested for this activity.

NUMBER RODS AND SMOOTH NUMERAL CARDS

The next activity is the Number Rods and Smooth Numeral Cards. The lesson involves counting and cardinality, and the child is taught the Common Core State Standard A1[36] "to know number names and the count sequence from 1–10 and transfer this knowledge to the KCCA3 standard."[37] The child also learns to represent a designated number of objects with a numeral.

Students begin the Number Rods and Smooth Numeral Card Activity after mastery of the Number Rods and Numeral Cards. This activity extends previously mastered numeral association of 1 to 9 to include numeral 10 and the associated Ten Rod.

First Period Lesson. This activity teaches the child to associate the Number Rods (concrete representation) with the Smooth Numeral Cards (abstract). For students who need additional support, the teacher brings the first three Number Rods (1, 2, 3) and Smooth Numeral Card (1, 2, 3) to the workspace in the same manner as previously mastered by the child in the Number Rod Activity. The teacher puts the Number Rods and the Smooth Numeral Cards back on the math shelf so the child can do the same thing while the teacher watches. If the teacher assesses that the child is capable of completing the entire "1" through "10" association during the initial instruction, the instruction will continue. If the three rods and numeral cards are obviously enough work for the child at this time, the teacher will wait and do more on another day. This accommodation is appropriate for all children in the classroom. Teachers should be very aware that the return of the Number Rods and Smooth Numeral Cards to their appropriate storage place is part of the activity.

The student who needs additional support may need to build up to the full Ten Rod Activity. However, after mastery of the Number Rods 1 to 4, the instructor should determine if the student is capable of going through all ten rods before moving onto the Second Period Lesson of the Number Rod and Smooth Numeral Card Activity. If the student demonstrates mastery of Number Rods 1–4 has been accomplished but movement to Number Rods 5–9 is creating a source of frustration, then the student should move through the Third Period Lesson with only Number Rods 1–4 and also continue to the Spindle Box Activity using only Number Rods 1–4.

Sensitivity to the success of the child is critical in order to prevent the repetition of an unsuccessful experience creating a feeling of learned helplessness. This activity requires teacher support and awareness of the limitations of the child's attention and patience (NAEYC 9).[38]

Second Period Lesson. During this lesson, the teacher observes whether the child chooses to perform the task independently. If the child does not demonstrate mastery of the concept during independent work, the teacher will re-present the lesson on another day.

Third Period Lesson. When appropriate, the teacher begins the summative assessment by asking the child, "What number is this?" The student who cannot answer this question should, on another day, revisit the First Period or Second Period Lessons with their teacher.

Individuals with Down syndrome may have a sense of numerosity but encounter primary difficulty with the numerical language activities. Children with Down syndrome typically may have a more skilled visual-spatial ability and therefore should manipulate the number rods before the teacher introduces the language. This is exactly how the number rods are introduced, and it is best practice for Down syndrome children.[39] Cardinality is a complex numerical concept that is not above the ability level of some individuals with Down syndrome. However, it does present a challenge.[40] Furthermore, young children with Down syndrome need clear task expectations and support to stay on task. Such support is essential for their success in early mathematical learning.[41] The use of creative instruction, clear expectations, and peer support in a Montessori setting is demonstrated in the following example.

Example 9: Suzie, a 3-year-old child with Down syndrome, carries the number rods to a mat not far from where the number rods are kept on the shelf. She has a good friend named Michael to help her focus. Michael is older than Suzie. When Suzie has finished her activity, she and Michael go to Suzie's special chart where they check off the work. Suzie checks on the right and Michael checks on the left. Michael gives Suzie a high five. They will work together again tomorrow.

SPINDLE BOX ACTIVITY

The natural progression of instruction following the Number Rod Activity is the Spindle Box Activity in which students experience counting spindles and the associated cardinality that lead to the discovery of the relationship between numbers and quantities. The symbols are in a fixed order from 0 to 9, and the wooden spindles are loose. Now the child must use the one-to-one counting principle to accurately count the forty-five spindles into their individual compartments. In a later lesson with the Spindle Boxes, "zero" is introduced. The absence of any quantity is a new and challenging concept for children, but one that needs to be firmly understood before continuing with either place value or linear counting. This progression is beneficial to all learners as it fosters generalization and transfer.

The child benefits from the direct instruction and opportunities for guided practice provided by the teacher in transferring the concepts of the Long Rod to the Spindle Box and then the Red Counter Activity.[42] The Spindle Box Activity is followed by the Red Wooden Counter Activity in which the child associates the correct number of objects with the smooth numeral cards.

RED WOODEN COUNTER ACTIVITY OR NUMERALS AND COUNTERS

First Period Lesson. To begin the Red Wooden Counter Activity, the teacher places the "1" numeral card on the mat as she places one red counter under the "1" numeral card. Then the teacher moves to the "2" numeral card and places two red counters under the two numeral cards and so on.

Second Period Lesson. Students will do the activity demonstrated by the teacher in the First Period by themselves, while telling the teacher what each numeral card represents. Following this demonstration of concept comprehension, students will continue the activity for numbers one through ten.

Third Period Lesson. During the summative assessment portion of the Red Counter Activity, the teacher points to the number and asks, "What is this?"

The student who needs additional support may need the Red Counter Activity divided into the numbers one through four, five through seven, and eight through ten. This differentiation allows the child to experience progression to move through the materials and concepts at a pace that maintains interest and dignity. After this method is used, the next activity will pair the red counters so "odd" and "even" can be introduced. The mastery of vocabulary can never be presumed as demonstrated in the following example.

Example 10: Myles is a 5-year-old boy with ADHD. During an activity reinforcing the language needed for math and the Red Wooden Counter Activity, Myles is asked to drop a "counter" on the floor. Myles reads the instructions on his card and walks to the practical life/kitchen area, picks a small counter (shelf), clears the shelves, and triumphantly drops the counter on the floor.

GEOMETRY CONCEPTS

Just as the Sensorial and Practical Life activities are going on while the child learns his or her beginning number concepts, early geometric concepts are also being explored in the early childhood Montessori environment. As in early math concepts, geometry lessons cover the Common Core Standards for KCCB.5[43] and K.G. Geometry.[44] To be more explicit, the Common Core Standards expect elementary children to identify and describe the shapes in table 4.1:[45]

Table 4.1.

Squares	Circles	Triangles
Rectangles	Hexagons	Cubes
Cones	Cylinders	Spheres

Early Geometry Activities complement the Sensorial Activities with the following lessons:

- The Tower of Cubes (or Pink Tower)
- Long Rods (or Red Rods)
- Broad Stairs (or Broad Prism)
- Knob Cylinders
- Knobless Cylinders

Visualization of dimension is presented through geometric solids known as the Broad Prisms (also known as Brown Stairs), Long Rods that change in length, and sets of cylinders (with and without knobs) that maintain height but change diameter *or* that maintain diameter but change height. The concept of geometry continues with the study of geometric solids. These lessons are activities that develop the child's visual and sensorial discrimination.

The geometric activities initially require more child observation by the teachers as the children work with the materials. Children are creating their own sense of spatial relationships through manipulation of the materials and learning the names of the geometric solids.[46]

GEOMETRIC SHAPES—
THREE-DIMENSIONAL GEOMETRIC SOLIDS

The first activity in the geometry series is the Visual Discrimination Activity. Children learn to recognize and name ten different three-dimensional geometric solids which are made of wood that is painted blue (table 4.2).

Although these terms seem advanced, the children have used them throughout Sensorial and some Practical Life activities and are not intimidated, for example, by the concept of a cube or cylinder; they have already

Table 4.2.

Cube	Ellipsoid
Sphere	Triangular prism
Cylinder	Rectangular prism
Ovoid	Square-based pyramid
Cone	Triangular-based pyramid

heard these words. Furthermore, these shapes have been available for free exploration in the sensorial environment for children as young as ages 3, 4, and 5 without the introduction of a formal lesson.[47] This provision of multiple means of engagement, which is the very beginning of transfer and generalization, is both important and very difficult for students with challenges.[48] It is critical to maximize transfer and generalization through direct instruction by a teacher.

First Period Lesson. In the Visual Discrimination of Form Activity, the child associates the geometric solid with the name of the shape through direct instruction by the teacher. The concept is traditionally introduced with three geometric solids: cube, sphere, and cylinder. Initially, the teacher hands the child the actual geometric solid and does not describe the form for the child using any words like "smooth," "sharp," and so on. The addition of verbal description can be very disruptive at this stage of learning for all children; it can be exceptionally disruptive for those children with challenges as it overloads the sensory input. Two of these three shapes (cubes and cylinders) were experienced earlier during the Sensorial Activities (the Tower of Cubes, the Cylinder Blocks, and the Knobless Cylinders). Cubes and cylinders have very different attributes. For example, the sharp corners of the cube are very different from the smooth round surface of the cylinder.[49] For the student who needs additional support, it may be necessary to start with two shapes previously experienced with the Tower of Cubes and the Cylinder Blocks and then introduce new shapes, like the sphere. During the initial presentation of geometric lessons, it is important for the teacher to avoid excessive conversation in order to allow all children to process the experience of the sensorial with the visual. It is particularly important for students who need additional support.[50]

Example 11: Ms. Laura asks a fifth-level student, Tim, to present two geometric solids (the cylinder and cube) to Ella. Tim first takes Ella to look at the Tower of Cubes and the Cylinder Blocks to remind Ella where the original learning experiences about the cylinder and cube took place. Ella has used the Cylinder Blocks and Tower of Cubes many times before. Then Tim sits with Ella and hands her the cube and the cylinder. Next, he asks Ella to pass the cube to him and then pass the cylinder to him. The next time they meet, Tim will repeat this exercise with the cube and cylinder and then add the sphere.

Second Period Lesson. the child is asked to differentiate between the two or three shapes that have been presented. The teacher makes the shapes available to the child and then asks the child to hand the requested shape to the teacher. There is an interplay following this activity to reinforce the correct terminology. For example, the teacher puts the cube and cylinder in a basket, covers it with a cloth, and asks the child to put his or her hand under the cloth. Then the teacher says to the child, "Please find and hand me the cube."

Third Period Lesson. When the child is successful with the Second Period Lesson, the teacher and child move to the Third Period Lesson. In this lesson, the teacher asks the child to identify the cube, sphere, and cylinder shapes when they are presented. Often an extended experience engages the child in identifying shapes in the environment that coincide with the geometric shapes they have learned. As an example, the teacher may ask the child if he or she can find a globe that looks like a sphere.[51] In this way, teachers can "recognize and build children's interest in making sense of their world through mathematics. They motivate children to learn math by connecting to real life, meaningful problems and situations."[52]

FLAT GEOMETRIC SHAPES

The lessons in the Geometric Cabinet are presented to pre-primary students in a specific order. The NAEYC 5 standard[53] and the State Content Standards[54] for early childhood require recognition of only four shapes:

Circle
Rectangle
Triangle
Quadrilaterals

If the child shows readiness, he or she can continue to:

regular polygons; and
curved figures.

In the Montessori classroom, the experience begins with the introduction to the Geometric Cabinet. The shapes are presented as puzzle pieces.

In a traditional 3–6 Montessori classroom, an overview tray sitting on top of the Geometric Cabinet includes three shapes: the circle, the square, and the triangle. However, in an inclusive classroom, the overview tray is not present; it is best to start with the circle tray contained in the Geometric Cabinet.[55] The teacher begins by introducing the largest circle and progressing through to the smallest of the six circles. During this exercise, the child learns to identify the circle and the order of size from largest to smallest. The circles are presented from the upper-left corner to the lower-right corner in order of size, from the three circles on the top row to the three on the bottom. This reinforces the same pattern that is used to read a page: left to right and top to bottom.

First Period Lesson. As the teacher removes each circle puzzle piece from the drawer one at a time, she names the shape for the child and runs her index finger around the shape. The idea here is to reinforce that the identity name "circle" is dependent only on shape, not size.

Example 12: Timmy has helped Lacy, who has autism, with other lessons; therefore, it is consistent for Ms. Laura to ask Timmy to present the geometry circle tray to Lacy, starting with the largest circle and progressing to the smallest circle. Timmy carefully takes the largest circle out of its frame inset with his left hand and traces the circle shape with his right index finger. Then Timmy traces the circle inset with his right index finger and places the circle back in the inset. Tracing the inset reinforces that the identity name "circle" is dependent only on shape, not size.

This process continues for all six circles. The child then returns each circle to the circle tray, and the tray is put back into the Geometric Cabinet.[56]

Second Period Lesson. The teacher asks the child to identify the circles. For students with challenges, the concept of what an object is *not* is just as important as what it *is*.[57] When the child can successfully pick out the circles from the circle tray, he or she is ready for the Third Period Lesson.

Third Period Lesson. The child responds when the teacher points to the circle and says, "What shape is this?"

The First, Second, and Third Period lessons are repeated using the rectangle tray and then the triangle tray. When working with each of the three trays, the child is not asked to differentiate between different shapes, but to recognize that each tray only contains all circles, all rectangles, or all triangles—even though the attributes of each circle, rectangle, or triangle may differ in size or length of sides. The child should be able to tell the teacher what each shape is called.

Some children may be ready to learn the detailed properties of the three shapes, including the relationship between numbers of sides, the names of the angles that are part of these shapes, and the names of each type of rectangle and triangle.

After the first three trays are mastered, the same Frist, Second, and Third Period Lesson formats are followed for each of the remaining three trays: quadrilaterals, regular polygons, and curved figures.

The Common Core State Standards for kindergarten-level children have many requirements for being able to compare geometric shapes.[58] Learning any language—including that of geometry—is easier at an early age than during the middle school years and beyond.

CONSTRUCTIVE TRIANGLE BOXES

The Constructive Triangle Boxes are presented after the children have learned the basic geometric shapes taught in the previous section.

The Triangle Box

First Period Lesson. The teacher begins presentation of the Constructive Triangle Box in the following way:

1. The teacher takes the child to the shelf in the geometry area of the classroom and brings the Triangle Box to the work carpet.
2. The teacher counts the sides of the Triangle Box with her index finger ("one, two, three") and says, "This three-sided figure is a triangle."
3. The child is shown how to use the color-coded puzzle pieces to construct each of three different equilateral triangles using the black lines on the side of the small triangles as guides. The black lines connect to form the green, yellow, and red equilateral triangles. On the sides of the small triangles are black lines.
4. The teacher constructs the green equilateral triangle, takes it apart, and puts the pieces back at the top of the work mat.

5. Then the child constructs the green equilateral triangle.
6. This process is repeated for the yellow and then the red equilateral triangles.
7. Next, the teacher and then the student will use a gray equilateral triangle from the same box to check their work. When the gray triangle is placed on top of the green, yellow, and red triangles, it will show they are congruent with the gray equilateral triangle.

For students who need additional support, the use of color "helps to increase the perceptual clarity and salience of information."[59] The number of pieces chosen for reassembly will depend upon the child's level of readiness. The child with challenges will do best starting with the triangle that can be constructed with the fewest pieces. In this box, the green equilateral triangle is constructed using only two right-angle triangles. This geometric exercise supports visual discrimination of form and the basis of congruency.

Example 13: The Constructive Triangle Box is presented to Lacy, who has autism, by Timmy. Timmy presents only one triangle at a time, starting with the two green triangles. After he takes out the two green pieces, he traces the black line on each green triangle with his right index finger and connects the two triangle pieces into one equilateral triangle. Timmy returns the two pieces to the box, and Lacy repeats this procedure. On another day with Lacy, Timmy will follow the same procedure to present, assemble, and disassemble the yellow and then the red triangle pieces. When Timmy completes the procedure for each colored triangle, Lacy will repeat the same procedures.

Second Period Lesson. When each child has mastered setting up and taking down the shapes in the Triangle Box,[60] the instructor teaches the formal names of the geometric shapes in the box to the child.

Third Period Lesson. The teacher points to each type of triangle and asks the child, "What kind of triangle is this?"

Although the Rectangle Boxes come after the Large and Small Hexagon Boxes in traditional Montessori classrooms, it is recommended the Large Hexagon Box and the Small Hexagon Box not be presented to students who have challenges until they have successfully assembled the Triangle and the Rectangle Boxes.

The Constructive Rectangle Box

Learning the concepts of discrimination of form and congruence continues with the First Rectangle Box.[61]

First Period Lesson. The teacher begins the lesson by introducing the child to the Rectangle Box itself. The teacher takes the child to the geometry shelf and brings the Rectangle Box to the work carpet or table. She counts the four sides of the Rectangle Box and says, "This is a rectangle." Note that although the box itself is four sided, it is also named "the Rectangle Box" because it contains a variety of triangle-shaped pieces that are used to make seven quadrilateral shapes taught in the Constructive Rectangle Box Activity:

Table 4.3.

2 yellow parallelograms	1 yellow rhombus	1 green parallelogram
1 red trapezoid	1 green square	1 gray rectangle

To continue the First Period Lesson:

1. The teacher takes the triangle-shaped pieces out of the Rectangle Box and sorts the triangles by color. Then the teacher puts the triangles back into the box and returns it to the geometry shelf.
2. The child is asked to carry the Rectangle Box to the mat and take out the triangles and sort them by color.
3. Next, the teacher constructs each of the seven shapes listed above from the triangle pieces, one at a time. After each quadrilateral is assembled and disassembled, she asks the child to assemble the same shape from the triangles. Each of the shapes is made in the same manner as the activities in the Triangle Box activity, using the black lines on each triangle as guides to create the shapes. The color-coded shapes are an extension of the triangle and show how two triangles can combine into a figure with four sides.
4. After the teacher constructs each shape, she teaches the child the formal name of the geometric shape, disassembles it, and asks the child to assemble the same shape from the triangles and then disassemble it.
5. This process is repeated for each of the seven shapes.

6. After the new shapes are made one at a time by a child with challenges, the teacher places the triangles back into the Rectangle Box and, with the child, returns the box to the geometry shelf where it was found.
7. Then the child brings the Rectangle Box to the work rug, makes the shapes, returns the triangle shapes to the Rectangle Box, and then takes it back to the shelf.[62]

Example 14: The Constructive Rectangle Box for Edward, who has ADHD, is presented by Ms. Laura, the teacher, who retrieves the box from the shelf, takes all the pieces out of the box, sorts them by color, and then returns all the pieces to the box. Next, Edward takes out all the pieces, sorts them into like colors, returns the pieces to the box, and puts the box back on the geometry shelf. During the next six weeks or so, Ms. Laura will assemble the pieces together in color piles one at a time until Edward can form all seven shapes from these color piles.

Second Period Lesson. When the child has demonstrated mastery of the First Period Lesson, the teacher asks the child to assemble the seven quadrilaterals and point to the correct shape as she names each one. ("Show me the rhombus.")

Third Period Lesson. The child is asked to construct all seven quadrilaterals and name each shape as the teacher points to it.[63] ("What shape is this?")

Large Hexagon Box

The next set of activities taught after the mastery of the Rectangle Box activities are those of the Large Hexagon-Shaped Box, which contains the following a mixture of equilateral and obtuse triangles:

1 yellow equilateral triangle (with black lines on all sides)
3 yellow obtuse isosceles triangles (with black lines opposite the obtuse angle)
2 red obtuse isosceles triangles (with black lines on the side opposite the obtuse angle)
2 gray obtuse triangles (with black lines on the shorter sides of the obtuse triangle)

First Period Lesson. The teacher introduces the Large Hexagon Box,[64] and sorts the triangle pieces it contains:

1. The teacher demonstrates feeling and counting the six sides of the box as she states, "This is a hexagon." It is important for all students—and definitely for those students needing additional support—that the teacher models putting her index finger on the first side of the Large Hexagon Box and then using her other index finger to count the other five sides.
2. In the next steps, the teacher opens the box, removes the triangle pieces, and sorts them by color (yellow, red, and gray). The teacher then selects the three yellow triangle pieces with two black lines on the shorter side. When the three pieces are isolated, she traces the lines with her index finger and joins the sides of the triangles to make an equilateral triangle.
3. While the teacher observes, the student repeats the procedure and places the constructed triangle on the upper left corner of the mat. *Note*: While constructed triangles are traditionally placed in the upper-left corner of the mat, this placement directive may introduce the concept "upper left," a complexity that might be best avoided at this time for the student needing additional support.

Example 15: Ms. Laura presents the Large Hexagon Box to Tim, a child who needs additional support. She brings the Hexagon Box to the mat and immediately places a large yellow dot on the upper-left corner of the mat. She shows Tim how to take the yellow triangles out of the box and put them together to make a hexagon, which she puts on top of the large yellow dot. Then she puts yellow pieces back in the box and Tim repeats what Ms. Laura demonstrated.

4. After removing the pieces used to form the equilateral triangle, the teacher takes all the remaining yellow triangles from the box and models how to join them to the large yellow equilateral triangle to form a hexagon. This is accomplished by putting the black lines on the three yellow obtuse triangles against the black lines on the large equilateral triangle.

Early Childhood Montessori Mathematical Education   71

5. After the teacher forms the hexagon, the student performs the activity with the teacher watching. Then the student places the hexagon next to the yellow triangle at the top of the mat. For the student who needs additional support, it might be wise to have pre-placed a small, yellow, six-sided hexagon (perhaps made of plastic or laminated paper) on the mat to guide placement.
6. Next, the teacher takes the two red obtuse triangles and connects them at the black lines to form a rhombus. Some students will recognize this shape as a rhombus from their work with the Rectangle Boxes.
7. The student then performs the activity with the teacher watching. For students who need additional support, the assembled red rhombus is placed on the red dot at the top of the mat.
8. The teacher then forms a parallelogram by taking the last two pieces (which are gray) and joining them at the black lines on the rhombus to form a parallelogram.
9. The student follows the example of the teacher to construct the parallelogram and places the figure next to the red rhombus at the top of the mat on a grey dot.
10. When the shapes have been made, the teacher should demonstrate how to put the wooden triangles back into the Large Hexagon Box. Then the teacher should put the pieces back on the mat and ask the child with challenges to put the pieces back in the box. After completing this work, the child is asked to put the Large Hexagon Box back on the shelf.

Second Period Lesson. Working with the individual children who have shown they are able to set up and take down the Large Hexagon Box, the instructor will teach all the formal names of the geometric figures made by the pieces in this box. While the student who needs additional support may not be ready to learn the names of all shapes, he or she can progress to this stage with those geometric figures that are mastered.

Third Period Lesson. This lesson, as described earlier in this chapter, is used to confirm the child can name each shape mastered in the Large Hexagon Box: triangle, hexagon, rhombus, and parallelogram. The mastery level must be carefully documented for each child so that the teacher can return to the First Period Lesson for those shapes not mastered.

Allowing the student who needs additional support to progress in this manner allows the student to experience a sense of accomplishment.

Small Hexagon Box

The Small Hexagon Box contains a combination of isosceles and obtuse triangles:

6 gray equilateral triangles (with black lines on two sides)
6 red obtuse isosceles triangles (with a black line on the side opposite the obtuse)
3 green equilateral triangles (two with black lines on one side and one with black lines on two sides)
2 red equilateral triangles (with a black line on one side)
1 yellow equilateral triangle (with no black lines)

Note: The obtuse red triangles are equal in size, and the red and green equilateral triangles are also equal in size.

First Period Lesson. To begin the lesson, the teacher takes the child to the geometry shelves, brings the Small Hexagon Box to the work mat, and identifies the shape of the box:

1. As with the Large Hexagon Box, the teacher feels and counts the sides of the box, saying "This is a hexagon. A hexagon has 6 sides." Then the child counts the sides.
2. The teacher takes all the triangles out of the box and sorts them according to color: red, gray, green, and yellow. When the teacher is working with a student needing additional support in an inclusive classroom, she returns the pieces to the box, puts it back on the shelf, and then invites the child to bring the Small Hexagon Box to the mat, count the sides, take out each piece, and sort them by color. Then the child puts the pieces back in the box and returns it to the geometry shelf.
3. In an inclusive classroom, the next visit to the Small Hexagon Box occurs after the child has been observed independently choosing the box, sorting the pieces by color, returning them to the box, and then to the shelf.[65] Varying the methods for response and navigation is best as

"learners differ widely in their optimal means for navigation through information and activities."[66]

4. At this point, the teacher repeats the cycle and adds the *construction* of the color shapes:

   - The gray pieces make a hexagon.
   - The red pieces make four rhombi.
   - The green pieces make a trapezoid.
   - The yellow equilateral triangle stands alone.

   Construction is aided by the dark lines on the shapes; the teacher traces the dark lines with her index finger as the shapes are assembled. After construction of each shape, the teacher places it on the dot of the same color at the top of the mat.

5. The child repeats the steps taken by the teacher to construct each shape: gray hexagon, four red rhombi, green trapezoid, and yellow equilateral triangle.
6. In an inclusive classroom, the teacher adds a step for each presentation by asking the child to make each shape and place it under the corresponding color dot on the mat (gray hexagon on the gray dot, four red rhombi on the red dot, etc.)
7. After completing this work, the child is expected to put the pieces back in the Small Hexagon Box and return the box to the geometry shelf.

The Second Period Lesson of the Small Hexagon Box is when the teacher works with individual children who have shown they can set up and take down the Small Hexagon Box to teach the formal names of all the geometric figures made by this box.[67] The Third Period Lesson, as described earlier in this chapter, will be used to teach hexagon, rhombus, trapezoid, and triangle.

Example 16: Ms. Laura invites Lacy, a child with autism, to watch her make the gray hexagon and place it on the gray dot at the top of the mat. Then Ms. Laura returns the gray pieces to the Small Hexagon Box and invites Lacy to repeat what she has done. On another day, Ms. Laura will continue teaching Lacy by showing her how to make three red rhombi and place them under the red dot at the top of the mat. Later, she will show Lacy how to make a green trapezoid and place it under the green dot.

Second Period Lesson. The teacher works with individual children who have shown they can set up and take down the Small Hexagon box to teach them the formal names of all the geometric figures made by this box. The child learns to touch the correct shape when the teacher asks, for example, "Where is the hexagon?"

Third Period Lesson. The teacher assesses the child's ability to assemble each of the seven colored shapes taught in the First Period Lesson and the child's ability to name them correctly when asked to do so by the teacher.

In the event the child cannot assemble the shapes in any of the Constructive Triangle Boxes with only a verbal prompt from the teacher, placing a picture of each shape on the bottom of each Constructive Triangle Box top can be an effective "control of error." In a UDL classroom, the teacher may offer descriptions of the process (if necessary) as well as a customized display of pre-drawn examples that can be used as a guide to follow.[68]

MATHEMATICS AND THE INCLUSIVE CLASSROOM

The lessons in this chapter provide examples of how the teacher should proceed with early math lessons, taking into consideration the need for differentiation of presentation and assessment for students who need additional support. Marie Montessori was the forerunner of the Four Principles of Maximizing the Effectiveness of Manipulatives:

1. Consistent use of manipulatives throughout mathematical education
2. Starting with concrete examples and moving to abstract concepts
3. Avoiding manipulatives that elicit dual representation
4. Directly explaining the relationship "between the manipulatives and the math concept"[69]

Montessori math materials are designed to offer students who need additional support an evidence-based method of instruction that decreases distraction and helps the child associate the manipulative with the mathematical concept it represents.[70] Everything about Montessori math is a continuum of known interrelated sequential relationships. For example, once the student understands the concept of numbers and cardinality of one to ten in the Red Wooden Counter Activity, the student can progress to the concrete Golden Bead material that presents the concepts of "unit," "ten," "hundred," and "thousand," which in turn leads to the decimal system. From that point, using the Golden Bead material leads to understanding addition, multiplication, subtraction, and division.

Maria Montessori was the first true special educator. In the early 1900s, her methods of instruction in mathematics used differentiated instruction and placed students who needed additional support side by side with their typical peers. Maria Montessori trusted the natural curiosity of all children. She believed that effective teaching assists the young child to advance on the way to independence.[71]

Henley, Ramsey, and Algozzine,[72] specialists in differentiation, state that effective teaching practices are universal. Montessori math teachers have instructional strategies that are time tested and universal. These strategies promote learning for the student who needs additional support, just as they do for students who do not have specific challenges.

Montessori in the early 1900s and Henley, Ramsey, and Algozzine in the early 2000s believed that the challenge is to change failure to success for every student. Early in the new millennium, Cecil Mercer, distinguished faculty member in education from the University of Florida, led a team that arrived at a similar strategy for teaching students who need additional support:

> Teachers are encouraged to time their interactions prescriptively so that they know when it is appropriate to provide direct instruction, give guided instruction, ask questions, offer corrective feedback, encourage, let the student work independently . . .ensure that students develop conceptual understanding—[and] are treated as active agents in their own learning."[73] Henley determined that students who need additional support "respond to the same instructional methods as other students. . . . They may require more time to achieve satisfactory levels of performance and typically require special instruction and extra practice to generalize."[74]

Early childhood mathematics in a Montessori classroom is designed to be proactive, to encourage extra practice, and to provide an instructional design that uses the function of each activity to allow for natural curiosity. Mathematics in the inclusive Montessori classroom can be a cherished experience, one where no child is excluded or left behind.

SUMMARY OF MATH STRATEGIES FOR SUPPORTING CHILDREN WITH LEARNING CHALLENGES

See table 4.4 for a summary of math strategies for supporting children with learning challenges.

Table 4.4.

Strategy	Description	Purpose
Re-presentation by a peer	A student selected by the teacher re-presents the lesson presented by the teacher.	Avoids the sense of failure that can inhibit self-esteem and discourage further learning by a child with learning challenges.
Maintaining the Prepared Environment	Always storing learning materials in their designated location.	Creates a sense of security and predictability that is helpful to all children.
Task achievement through partnership with a peer	Example: When a snack is to be given after a card is read, a child who can read is partnered with a child who cannot.	Avoids the sense of failure that can inhibit self-esteem and discourage further learning by a child with learning challenges.
Accommodating different learning style preferences	Using picture prompts to support children who need additional support and who respond to visual assistance	Encourages success, which supports additional learning.
Limiting quantity of materials or stimuli presented at one time	Introduction of pieces of an activity one at time. Avoiding using of extensive verbiage (such as "left-hand bottom corner") during a presentation.	Reduces distraction for children who need additional support.
Accommodating physical challenges	Reducing the number of items and/or distance items are to be carried when a child has physical challenges, such as sitting in a wheelchair.	Encourages success, which supports additional learning.
Accommodating excess sensitivity to textures (e.g., rough sandpaper)	Use smooth numerical cards or make cards out of felt.	Alleviates discomfort some children experience when handling rough textures.

NOTES

1. NAEYC, "Early Childhood Mathematics: Promoting Good Beginnings," 2002, 2010, 3, last modified 2010, https://www.NAEYC.org/files/NAEYC/file/positions/psmath,pdf .

2. Ibid.

3. American Academy of Pediatrics Subcommittee on ADHD Disorder. *ADHD: Clinical Practice Guidelines for the Diagnosis, Evaluation, and Treatment of Attention Deficit Hyperactive Disorder in Children and Adolescents*, 2011.

4. E. M. Standing. *Maria Montessori: Her Life and Work* (New York: New American Library of World Literature, 1962).

5. CAST, *Universal Design for Learning Guidelines Version 2.0* (Wakefield, MA: Author, 2011). Principle III, Guideline 8, Checkpoint 8.2, 31.

6. National Autistic Society, *Obsessions Repetitive Behavior and Routine*, http://www.autism.org.uk.

7. CAST, *Universal Design for Learning*, Principle III, Guideline 7, Checkpoint 7.3, 29.

8. Standing, *Maria Montessori*, 271.

9. NAEYC, "Early Childhood Mathematics," 4–5.

10. Maria Montessori, *Maria Montessori: The Discovery of the Child* (New York: Ballantine Books, 1967).

11. NAEYC, "Early Childhood Mathematics," 5–6.

12. Ibid., 4.

13. CAST, *Universal Design for Learning*, Principle III, Guideline 8, Checkpoint 8.1, 30.

14. Ibid., Principle II, Guideline 4, Checkpoint 4.1, 22.

15. Ibid., Principle I, Guideline 1, Checkpoint 1.1, 14.

16. Maria Montessori, *The Montessori Method* (New York: Schocken Books, 1964), 194.

17. CAST, *Universal Design for Learning*, Principle III, Guideline 7, Checkpoint 7.1, 28.

18. NAEYC, "Early Childhood Mathematics," 5.

19. Maria Montessori, *Maria Montessori: The Secret of Childhood* (New York: Ballantine Books, 1979), 42.

20. CAST, *Universal Design for Learning*, Principle I, Guideline 1, Checkpoint 1.2, 15.

21. NAEYC, "Early Childhood Mathematics," 6.

22. Standing, *Maria Montessori*, 307.

23. A. S. Lillard, *Montessori: The Science Behind the Genius* (New York: Oxford University Press, 2005). 178.

24. C. D. Mercer and P. Pullen, *Students with Learning Disabilities* (Upper Saddle River, NJ: Pearson, 2005).

25. Montessori, *The Montessori Method*, 177–78.

26. NAEYC, "Early Childhood Mathematics," 9.

27. Montessori, *Education and Peace* (United States: Henry Regnery Company, 1972), 20.

28. NAEYC, "Early Childhood Mathematics," 6.

29. Common Core State Standards: Kindergarten Math Standards, 2019, 1, accessed September 21, 2019, https://www.ixl.com/printstandards/?state=cc&stds.

30. CAST, *Universal Design for Learning*, Principle II, Guideline 5, Checkpoint 5.3, 24.

31. Eileen Raymond, *Learners with Mild Disabilities: A Characteristic Approach* (Boston: Pearson, 2002). 258.

32. CAST, *Universal Design for Learning*, Principle II, Guideline 4, Checkpoint 4.1, 22.

33. Common Core State Standards: Kindergarten Math Standards, 3.

34. K. Michelle Lane-Barmapox, *Montessori and Autism: An Interpretive Description Study.* (Alberta, Canada: Athabasca University, 2016), 33.

35. CAST, *Universal Design for Learning*, Principle III, Guideline 3, Checkpoint 3.2, 20.

36. Common Core State Standards: Kindergarten Math Standards, 1–3.

37. Ibid.

38. NAEYC, "Early Childhood Mathematics," 9.

39. V. Camos. "Numerosity Discrimination in Children with Down Syndrome." *Developmental Neuropsychology* 34, no. 4 (2009), 435–47, 435.

40. Ibid.

41. R. Bull, K. A. Espy, and S. A. Wiebe. "Short-Term Memory, Working Memory, & Executive Functioning in Preschoolers: Longitudinal Predictors of Mathematical Achievement at Age 7 Years." *Developmental Neuropsychology* 33, no. 3, (2007), 205–28.

42. CAST. *Universal Design for Learning*, Principle III, Guideline 7, Checkpoint 7.1, 28–29.

43. Common Core State Standards: Kindergarten Math Standards, 3.

44. Ibid., K.G. Geometry, 6–7.

45. Ibid., K.G.A. Geometry, 6.

46. NAEYC, "Early Childhood Mathematics," 8.

47. Ibid., 8.

48. CAST, *Universal Design for Learning*, Principle I, Guideline 3, Checkpoint 3.4, 20.

49. NAEYC, "Early Childhood Mathematics," 8.

50. CAST, *Universal Design for Learning*, Principle I, Guideline 3, Checkpoint 3.3, 20.

51. NAEYC, "Early Childhood Mathematics," 7.

52. Carol Copple and Sue Bredekamp, eds. *Developmentally Appropriate Practice in Early Childhood Programs Serving Children from Birth through Age 8*, third edition (Washington, DC: NAEYC, 2013), 313.

53. NAEYC, "Early Childhood Mathematics," 6.

54. Common Core State Standards: Kindergarten Math Standards, K.G.A. Geometry, 6.

55. CAST. *Universal Design for Learning*, Principle I, Guideline 3, Checkpoint 3.2, 19.

56. Ibid., Principle 1, Guideline 1, Checkpoint 1.1, 14.

57. James McLeskey et al. *High-Leverage Practices in Special Education* (Arlington, VA: Council for Exceptional Children & CEEDAR Center, 2017).

58. Common Core State Standards: Kindergarten Math Standards, K.G.B.4, 6.

59. CAST, *Universal Design for Learning*, Principle I, Guideline 1, Checkpoint 1.1, 19.

60. Common Core State Standards: Kindergarten Math Standards, K.G.A.2 (K-V.3), 6.

61. Common Core State Standards: Kindergarten Math Standards, K.G.A.2. (K-V.5), 6.

62. CAST, *Universal Design for Learning*, Principle I, Guideline 1, Checkpoint 1.3, 15 (offer alternatives for visual information).

63. NAEYC, "Early Childhood Mathematics," 9.

64. Common Core State Standards: Kindergarten Math Standards, K.G.A.2 (K-V.6), 6.

65. CAST, *Universal Design for Learning*, Principle II, Guideline 4, Checkpoint 4.1, 22.

66. Ibid., Principle III, Guideline 3, Checkpoint 3.2, 22.

67. Common Core State Standards: Kindergarten Math Standards, K.G.A.2 (K-V.6), (K-W.7), 6.

68. CAST, *Universal Design for Learning*, Principle I, Guideline 1, Checkpoint 1.1 & 1.3, 14,15.

69. E. V. Laski, J. R. Jor'dan, C. Daoust, and A. K. Murray. "What Makes Mathematics Manipulatives Effective? Lessons from Cognitive Science and Montessori Education," 2, accessed October 1, 2019, http://www.uk.sagepub.com/aboutus/openaccess.htm,2015, 2.

70. Ibid., 3.

71. Montessori, *Maria Montessori: The Discovery*.

72. M. Henley, R. S. Ramsey, and R. F. Algozzine, *Characteristics of the Strategies for Teaching Students with Mild Disabilities* (Boston: Pearson, 2006).
73. C. D. Mercer, A. R. Mercer, and P. C. Pullen. *Teaching Students with Learning Problems* (Boston: Pearson, 2011), 411.
74. Henley, Ramsey, and Algozzine, *Characteristics of the Strategies*, 116.

BIBLIOGRAPHY

American Academy of Pediatrics Subcommittee on ADHD Disorder. *ADHD Clinical Practice Guidelines for the Diagnosis, Evaluation and Treatment of Attention Deficit Hyperactive Disorders in Children and Adolescents.* Accessed January 25, 2020. https://pediatrics.aapublications.org/content/128/5/1007, 2011.

Bull, Rebecca, Kimberly Andrews Espy, and Sandra A. Wiebe. "Short-Term Memory, Working Memory, & Executive Functioning in Preschoolers: Longitudinal Predictors of Mathematical Achievement at Age 7 Years." *Developmental Neuropsychology* 33, no. 3 (2007), 205–28.

Camos, Valerie. "Numerosity Discrimination in Children with Down Syndrome." *Developmental Neuropsychology* 34, no. 4 (2009), 435–47.

Carbonneau, Kira J., Scott C. Marley, and James P. Selig. "A Meta-analysis of the Efficacy of Teaching Mathematics with Concrete Manipulatives." *Journal of Educational Psychology* 105 (2013), 380–400.

CAST, *Universal Design for Learning Guidelines Version 2.0*, 2011. Wakefield, MA: Author. Accessed January 24, 2020. http://www.cast.org/our-work/about-udl.html.

Common Core State Standards: Kindergarten Math Standards, 1. Accessed September 21, 2019, https://www.ixl.com/printstandards/?state=cc&stds.

Copple, Carol, and Sue Bredekamp, eds. *Developmentally Appropriate Practice in Early Childhood Programs Serving Children from Birth through Age 8.* Washington, DC: NAEYC, 2013.

Henley, Marin, Robert S. Ramsey, and Robert F. Algozzine. *Characteristics of the Strategies for Teaching Students with Mild Disabilities.* Boston: Pearson, 2006.

Lane-Barmapox, K. Michelle. "Montessori and Autism: An Interpretive Description Study." Master's thesis, Athabasca University, Canada, 2016.

Laski, Elida V., Jamilah R. Jor'dan, Carolyn Daoust, and Angela K. Murray. "What Makes Mathematics Manipulatives Effective? Lessons from Cognitive Science and Montessori Education." Sages and Open Access. Accessed March 4, 2018. https://www.uk.sagepub.com/aboutus/openaccess.htm.

Lillard, Angeline Stoll. *Montessori: The Science behind the Genius.* New York: Oxford University Press, 2005.

McKenzie, Ginger Kelley, and Victory S. Zascavage. "Montessori Instruction: A Model for Inclusion in Early Childhood Classrooms and Beyond." *Montessori Life* 24, no. 1 (2012), 32–38.

McLeskey, James, Barringer, Mary Dean Barringer, Bonnie Billingsley, Mary Browness, Dia Jackson, Michael Kennedy et al. *High-Leverage Practices in Special Education.* Arlington, VA: Council for Exceptional Children & CEEDAR Center, 2017.

Mercer, Cecil D., Ann R. Mercer, and Paige C. Pullen. *Teaching Students with Learning Problems.* Boston: Pearson, 2011.

Mercer, Cecil D., and Paige C. Pullen. *Students with Learning Disabilities.* Upper Saddle River, NJ: Pearson, 2005.

Meyer, Anne, David H. Rose, and David Gordon. *Universal Design for Learning: Theory and Practice.* Wakefield, MA: CAST, 2014. http://www.cast.org.

Montessori, Maria. *Education and Peace.* United States: Henry Regnery Company, 1972.

Montessori, Maria. *Maria Montessori: The Discovery of the Child.* New York: Ballantine Books, 1967.

Montessori, Maria. *Maria Montessori: The Secret of Childhood.* New York: Ballantine Books, 1979.

Montessori, Maria. *The Montessori Method.* New York: Schocken Books, 1964.

NAEYC. "Early Childhood Mathematics: Promoting Good Beginnings," 2002, 2010. Accessed October 2, 2018, https://www.NAEYC.org/files/NAEYC/file/positions/psmath.pdf.

National Autistic Society, *Obsessions Repetitive Behavior and Routine.* Accessed February 5, 2019. http://www.autisium.org.uk.

National Council of Teachers of Mathematics. *Principles and Standards for School Mathematics.* Accessed April 4, 2018. https://www.nctm.org/astandards-and-positions/principles-and-standards.

Raymond, Eileen. *Learners with Mild Disabilities: A Characteristic Approach.* Boston: Pearson, 2002.

Standing, E. M. *Maria Montessori: Her Life and Work.* New York: New American Library of World Literature, 1962.

Zascavage, Victoria, and Kathy Winterman. "Assistive Technology and Universal Design for Learning: What Does the Middle School Educator Need to Know?, *Middle School Journal* 40 no. 4 (2009), 46–52.

Chapter Five

Montessori Language Practices Meet the Needs of All Learners

The Montessori Early Childhood Inclusive Classroom: Creating a Cherished Experience

Vanessa M. Rigaud

The Universal Design Learning (UDL) framework has received considerable scholarly attention within the past four years.[1] The latest reform, the Every Student Succeeds Act (ESSA) of 2015, specified numerous requirements to support students with learning challenges and included the use of the UDL framework (114 U.S.C. §1005).[2] The previously forgotten, ignored, overlooked, and disabled children of our society are no longer isolated; they now are included in the rich mosaic student population in general classrooms around the world today.

Laws have been developed and established to protect the rights of children with disabilities; however, current literature shows that teachers are facing challenges with their new inclusive environments.

In the public education sector, the ratio of children needing additional support continues to increase as educational systems around the world work hard to integrate all children in general education classrooms, providing new training and resources and setting high expectations for learning outcomes. Montessori teachers, like many others in the field, wrestle with facilitating instruction for the wide assortment of student needs in the classroom.

This chapter investigates the alignment of the Early Childhood (EC) Montessori language curriculum with the UDL framework and the National Association for the Education of Young Children (NAEYC). In the first section of this chapter, the Montessori holistic language curriculum will be outlined to establish a deeper understanding of the curricular components and materials used for language instruction.

The other four sections will focus on the alignment of the Montessori holistic language curriculum within the UDL framework, giving practitioners concrete examples of how explicit differentiation affords children with disabilities equitable access to literacy:

1. Early Preparations for Language Development in the Montessori Classroom for All Children
2. Exercises for the Hand: Fine Motor Preparation for Writing
3. Exercises for Phoneme, Graphemes, and Correspondence Preparation
4. Exercises for Reading

Additionally, this chapter will provide concrete strategies and lesson adaptations for effective teaching in the Montessori EC environment. These strategies and tools integrate a variety of modalities, thus minimizing obstacles to learning while providing opportunities for all children to succeed.[3]

The chapter will serve as a guide in preparing Montessori lessons for a diverse group of learners in the area of language development. At the end of the chapter, table 5.1 illustrates the UDL adaptations to the Montessori language lessons that are discussed in this chapter.

MONTESSORI HOLISTIC LANGUAGE PROGRAM FOR EARLY CHILDHOOD CHILDREN

Dr. Montessori worked in the education of children with disabilities in the late 1800s and early 1900s, which makes her a pioneer in this area. All of Dr. Montessori's prior work informed her conviction that educating the child begins at birth.[4]

She believed that babies obtained language from careful observation of their natural environment. Babies absorbs language from the womb, and then two months after birth, they begin to produce "'ca'—a meaningless phoneme," which begins the miracle of language – babbling.[5] The parents' responses encourage an increase in babbling as the baby practices hearing and creating sound.

Hearing the simple names of objects and activities lays the foundation for intellectual interaction to happen. Thus, the baby connects meaning to sounds that he hears around him.[6] By twelve months, the baby has learned about six words. When fifty words have been acquired, an explosion of language occurs with "the metabolic activity and synapse formation of the cerebral cortex."[7]

Within the next six years of life, the toddler will obtain a new vocabulary word every two waking hours. Following the acquisition of substantive words (nouns), the child launches into the use of all kinds of words—verbs, prepositions, adjectives, and adverbs—which primes the explosion of sentences.

This victorious crescendo of linguistic development opens the doors to expression and communication.[8] The child is learning at his own rhythm and speed. In this structure, the child learns to concentrate on each essential step in language so that a gradual step is achieved effortlessly, without any contemplation on the part of the child.[9] The child's spontaneous activity allows him to master the original "mother tongue" language without books or lessons.[10]

Dr. Montessori wanted to take advantage of this absorption of language in the EC Montessori classroom. To do this, she created a rich prepared environment to surround the child with a mosaic landscape nomenclature of the world. She utilized didactic materials that guided children to learn independently within a clinical environment. Dr. Montessori designed the materials and gave strong directives for implementing them in classroom environments.

The curriculum leads to the initiation of training programs that transmit her philosophy and methods of education to teachers.[11] These unique materials also play an essential role in aiding the child to develop the powers of communication and expression, organization, and classification—as well as the ability to think.

Dr. Montessori believed that children must understand and have concrete experiences that inform them about their world. That knowledge is obtained through various motor explorations and sensorial experiences.

The foundation of language is built through the senses: sight, hearing, touch, taste, and smell. The child learns to sort, classify, and store information about her environment in an orderly fashion. Training the senses assists her in the development of pre-linguistic skills, prerequisites for symbolic language development.[12]

The Montessori EC curriculum consists of five content areas: Practical life, sensorial, mathematics, language, and cultural. Montessori contended that language should develop organically while guiding the child with developmentally appropriate didactic materials.[13] In Montessori education, language development begins with the initial lesson in practical life. Sensorial is later woven into all areas of the curriculum. The teacher trains the child's ear with clear and precise speech that provides nomenclature related to the exercise, leaving out extraneous concepts.[14]

In the Three Period Lesson, the teacher guides the child to the vocabulary that is used to identify the object, compare it to other objects, and recognize differences. The Three Period Lesson consists of three parts:

- First period: Naming
- Second period: Recognition
- Third period: Pronunciation of the word[15]

Through various exercises in practical life and sensorial, the child prepares the mind and the hand. These experiences allow for words to be fixed to ideas that then can facilitate the comprehension of knowledge and vocabulary.[16]

NAEYC has played a dynamic role in developing standards for the early childhood curriculum used across the United States. The standards and desired outcomes align with the Montessori EC curriculum and support children with various learning challenges. NAEYC Standard 2, Sections D and E provide the scaffold for early literacy programs nationwide.[17] Considerable advancements have been achieved in the area of language development and literacy, but challenges remain.[18]

EARLY PREPARATIONS FOR LANGUAGE DEVELOPMENT FOR ALL CHILDREN

NAEYC Standard 2, Section D (Language Development) "addresses program plans and materials for supporting children's language development. The goals and objectives for language acquisition address both verbal and nonverbal communication and are rooted in ethnic and other community traditions."[19] Listening, talking, reading, and writing are all parts of early literacy learning and are wonderfully connected in the Montessori EC classroom.

The initial language materials in the Montessori EC environment are specifically chosen to aid in the refinement of visual acuity, commencing with matching:

- objects to objects;
- objects in the environment;
- objects to pictures; and
- pictures to pictures.

Matching exercises also include use of cards, which children use to match:

- whole to part;
- graphic representation;
- part to whole; and
- classification.[20]

The matching activities allow children to define and classify a multitude of impressions. The impression is then attached to an object or photo, giving the child a clear and precise vocabulary for the impression. In these exercises are found essential elements for language development: the ability to make associations and to categorize objects through impressionistic images created in the brain.

Though bewildering to the outsider, many of these activities are located in other curricular areas such as practical life, sensorial, cultural studies, math, and cultural (botany, zoology, history, geography, and physical science). Dr. Montessori intentionally embedded early language experiences throughout the curriculum. She understood that these materials would awaken the child's curiosity while preparing the visual, motor, lingual, and auditory centers of the brain for the integration of systems leading to success in future reading and writing.[21]

The Object in the Environment Nomenclature Activity lesson in the EC Montessori classroom provides visual discrimination and oral development while building vocabulary. Five small objects from the classroom are collected in a basket.

In the First Period Lesson, the teacher removes an object from the basket one at a time. The teacher says its name ("This is a teacup.") and places it on the rug. She continues in this fashion for the first three objects.

In the Second Period Lesson, the teacher says the name of each object on the rug, and the child points to the object.

In the Third Period Lesson, the teacher points to an object and asks the child to say its name. If the child can correctly name and identify the three objects, the teacher introduces two more to the group and repeats the process of the Three Period Lesson.

Modification Example 1: John, a 3.5-year-old, joins the Montessori EC classroom for the first time. He is new to Montessori but has attended a local daycare in the area. His teacher, Ms. Kate, realizes after the first week that his language vocabulary is minimal, and the school's initial assessments indicate there are some language delays at this time. Ms. Kate decides to give a lesson on "objects in the environment" to build vocabulary. Ms. Kate uses the Three Period Lesson to name each object, practice attaching the name to the object, and then assesses John's ability to use the name to identify the objects.

According to Michael Graves, "promoting the development of word consciousness and using wordplay activities to motivate and engage students in learning new words" helps children develop a rich, robust vocabulary that supports understanding texts containing those words.[22]

"What Is Missing?" is a vocabulary game that uses objects to provide opportunities for visual and auditory discrimination, use of memory, and preparation for writing and reading. To begin, the teacher builds a tray with five different spoons. She introduces the child to the different kinds of spoons, naming each spoon and describing how each kind of spoon is used. Then she places the spoons in a horizontal line (left to right and top to bottom) in front of the child. As the teacher says the name of each spoon, the child is asked to point to it.

Next, the teacher places a large cloth napkin over all the spoons. She asks the child to cover his eyes while she removes one of the spoons and places it on the tray under a second napkin.

Finally, the teacher removes the napkin covering the spoons and asks, "What is missing?" The child examines the remaining spoons and tries to identify which one is missing. The game continues in this manner until the child can recall all the names of the spoons and determine the missing one.

The next lessons follow a precise sequence that builds the child's understanding of a word from object name to abstract meaning.

The teacher begins with the object-to-object matching lessons for a few weeks, followed by object-to-picture matching the next couple of weeks. Next is naming objects in the environment and picture-to-picture matching. The sequence concludes with picture-to-label matching after the child has grasped the concepts in the previous lessons.[23]

This visual representation correlates directly with UDL strategies.[24] It allows the child to obtain a visual image to connect to a word, which leads them to comprehension.

The child is self-invigorated to partner with another child so they can share the new vocabulary and understanding obtained in the lesson, demonstrating the use of the Principle of Action and Expression in the UDL.[25] The object and pictures in matching materials spark interest among the children, encouraging them to engage more fully in the activity.

The children enjoy the option of practicing with a peer and developing fluency with the materials. Therefore, children can "build fluencies with graduated levels of support for practice and performance" with vocabulary, a concept found under the UDL Principle of Action and Expression, Guideline 5: Expression and Communication, Checkpoint 5.3.[26]

To help children learn to classify objects in the environment and develop spoken language, Dr. Montessori developed classified cards. The classified cards begin with matching one object to a specific topic (such as plants or animals). The exercise gradually changes to involve the children in the more complex task of sorting objects into two different topics.[27] The teacher prepares several sets for "Things That Go Together" activities in advance and introduces a new set each week.

Classifying these cards gives the child an opportunity to manipulate the cards and construct knowledge through relationships, which aligns beautifully with the UDL Principle of Representation and Engagement, Guideline 8: Sustaining Effort and Persistence, Checkpoint 8.3: Foster Collaboration and Community. Through their collaborative work, children "Construct communities of learners engaged in common interests or activities."[28] Working with a partner sustains the child's motivation and permits the exchange of understanding and language.[29]

EXERCISES FOR THE HAND: FINE MOTOR PREPARATION FOR WRITING

NAEYC has established the following standard to support the young child's physical development of gross and fine motor skills: "Curriculum Standard 2.C. Physical development - addresses program plans, materials, and equipment for the support of children's large motor development."[30] In the Montessori EC environment, the education of movement is a system of practices that lead to the external appearance of "discipline" of the body, which later advances to fine motor development of the hand.[31]

The preparation for the movement of the hand has been previously developed through practical life and sensorial experiences in the EC environment. Now the child must acquire the management of the hand as an instrument of writing.[32]

To this end, Dr. Montessori created a variety of materials, beginning with the geometric metal insets. The insets are displayed on two sloping wooden boards, each consisting of five pink, square metal frames. Inset in each frame is a two-dimensional, blue geometric figure.

Each inset shape has a knob located in the center. The geometric metal insets aid in acquiring the fine motor skill required to manage a writing instrument. The following activity also allows the child to discover that varying the amount of pressure applied with the pencil creates different line qualities (light, even, dark, etc.)

The teacher selects one metal inset shape, places the frame and inset on a tray with one five-and-a-half-inch square piece of paper and two colored pencils. The teacher brings the tray to the table. Next, the teacher places the frame over the piece of paper, aligning it so that it covers the paper's edge perfectly. Then, the teacher selects one of the colored pencils and traces the inside of the frame beginning from the top left corner.

The teacher removes the frame and now places the inset within the colored line drawn on the paper, aligning it so the figure is hidden. Then, the inset is traced using the other colored pencil, again starting from the upper-left corner again. When the activity is complete, the paper has two colored contours made on it.

Modification Example 2: Sky is a 5-year-old child in a Montessori EC classroom. She has been at the school for two years. She was recently diagnosed with autism. Sky seems impatient and unwilling to complete any task. Ms. Kate notices that Sky is attracted to the art area. She is often drawn to the colored pencils and enjoys watching the older children draw.

Since Sky has a developing pincher grip now and stronger fine motor control, Ms. Kate gives her a lesson on the metal insets. Ms. Kate uses the square metal frame in the initial lesson. Ms. Kate tells Sky to say aloud, "Slow . . . slow . . . slowly I control my hand" as she traces inside the frame.

Sky is excited and begins making her inset drawing immediately. She is captivated by being able to make many different figures on the paper. Sky is motivated and completes ten designs in two days. With each one she completes, her pincer grip is refined. After two weeks, Ms. Kate introduces the inset and frame together.

Providing ten colored pencils designated for this material and allowing the child to choose only two at a time sets a framework for exploration.[33] This option for choice provides children the opportunity to discover color combinations while arousing the desire to repeat the activity several times using two different colors.[34]

When the child has completed several designs, he can create an inset booklet that can be shared with others.[35] Usually, after the child has completed eight or more outlines and created a booklet with the designs, the teacher will give the next lesson, in which he learns how to fill in the outline.

The second presentation adds to the children's excitement. The teacher models how to fill in the outline with straight vertical lines, moving from left to right and top to bottom. This activity offers options for "increasing perceptual clarity," a concept found in the UDL Principle of Representation, Guideline 1: Perception, Checkpoint 1.3: Offer Alternatives for Visual Information.[36] While learning samples of design sequenced from simplest to the most complex, children enhance their fine motor skills as they conceptualize various shapes through a sensorial experience.[37]

Dr. Montessori also created a set of sandpaper letters that include the lowercase alphabet, the uppercase alphabet, and phonograms. The alphabet wooden card sets are designed in two colors: A sandpaper imprint of vowels and wooden board in pink and a sandpaper imprint of consonants and wooden board in blue. The phonogram set is all green.

The teacher selects a sandpaper letter and places it on a tray with a low-rim wooden box containing sand or cornmeal and a small towel folded next to the box. The tray is placed on the table. The teacher takes the sandpaper letter and places it to the left of the tray. She traces the sandpaper letter with the middle and index fingers of her dominant hand.

Then the teacher traces the same letter in the sand or cornmeal in the box. She admires her work with a smile. Next, she removes any sand remaining on her fingers by gently rubbing them together above the tray and then wipes them on the towel. She invites the child to trace the sandpaper letter and then trace the same shape in the box containing sand or cornmeal. Later, the child will transition from forming letters with her finger in sand to using chalk on the chalkboard and then to using a pencil on lined paper.

This transition is vital for the development of hand for writing. The UDL directs educators to "provide graphic symbols with alternative text descriptions" that offer "a graphic image that carries meaning" with representation of the letter (Principle of Representation, Guideline 2: Language and Symbols, Checkpoint 2.1). Children's fine motor skills are refined as they conceptualize various letters shapes through a tactile experience.[38]

EXERCISES FOR PHONEME, GRAPHEMES, AND CORRESPONDENCE PREPARATION

The Early Literacy section of the NAEYC Standard 2 "addresses program plans and materials for supporting early literacy through reading, learning letters and sounds, writing, and immersion in a print-rich environment."[39] The sandpaper letters activities found in the Montessori EC environment offer visual and auditory representation of the sound while giving children opportunities to perform hand movements necessary for writing letters, as discussed earlier.

This set of large alphabet cards has one glued sandpaper outline of each letter mounted on a board. Consonant sounds are blue, and vowels are red.[40] Using the card, the teacher introduces the child to two different sounds, connecting prior knowledge of names as she follows the format of the Three Period Lesson:

- "Remember when we were saying our names? Your name is 'Tricia.' 'Tricia' starts with the "t" sound. Well, I am going to show you what the 'T' sound looks like."

- The teacher shows the "T" sandpaper letter and says, "Now I am going to show you how to write it."
- The teacher models how to trace the letter with the right index and middle finger of her dominant hand, and then says the sound.
- She has the child trace the letter three times, saying the sound after each tracing. Then she places the sandpaper letter face up in the left corner of the table.
- The teacher introduces the second letter similarly to the first. The teacher continues with the Three Period Lesson.
- When the child has finished the exercise, the teacher replaces the tablets and repeats this lesson on consecutive days.[41]

When the child has learned the letters "s," "m," "t," and "a," the teacher gives the next series of the lessons, in which she combines two consonant letter sounds with the vowel "a" to form consonant-vowel-consonant (CVC) words. The teacher points the sandpaper letter, says the sound, slides to the next letter, and says the next letter sound. She continues in this fashion with the following letter, producing the word. The teacher models how to read words that can be formed with these four letters: "Sam," "mat," "sat," "at," and "tam."

Modification Example 3: Tricia, a 3.7-year-old, attends the Daisy Cottage Montessori EC classroom. She was born in the United States, but she has been speaking Korean since the age of two. Tricia is shy and reluctant to speak in public. She has limited English proficiency. When spoken to in private, Tricia seems to express herself with short sentences; however, some sounds are not well articulated, and it is hard to make out what she is saying.

Ms. Kate noticed that she completes all her work and shows an interest in reading. Ms. Kate presents the sandpaper letters to help Tricia with the initial phonetic sounds of the letters in the English language. Within a few weeks, Ms. Kate sees improvement with the "B," "T," and "H" sounds, which brings clarity to what Tricia is saying when speaking.

Three sensations are acquired through this lesson experience: sight, touch, and kinesthetic (muscular) sensation.[42] The use of sandpaper letters serves multiple objectives in that it provides visual recognition of letters, kinesthetic recognition of letters, and phonetic sound of letters and it also trains the hand in the light touch needed for writing. By providing a graphic symbol that can be attached to sound and later to words, this adaptation for a child in Montessori EC classroom supports the UDL Principle of Representation, Guideline 2: Language and Symbols, Checkpoint 2.2: "Clarify vocabulary and symbols."[43]

In the EC Montessori classroom environment, the moveable alphabet is used to introduce the child to writing words, thoughts, and sentences with graphic symbols, even if the hand is not ready to write. The moveable alphabet is placed in a shallow wooden box that has compartments for each letter. Each letter is a carved wooden piece that matches the sandpaper letters previously introduced.

During the lesson, the teacher dictates words that are spelled out by the child. The child finds each letter in the moveable letter alphabet box that represents each sound and places it on the mat to form the word.[44] The objective of this activity is to show the child that one is able to form words by matching sound to visual recognition of letters. Following is an example of how the sandpaper letters and moveable alphabet letters can be used to assist a child who needs additional support.

Modification Example 4: Steven is a new 5.2-year-old child in the Montessori EC classroom. He has dysgraphia and does not show interest in reading or writing. Steven avoids work that requires him to write but loves to work with the sandpaper letters and often goes to the reading corner. Ms. Kate selects the moveable alphabet lesson to present today and gives him photos of CVC words to spell out with the movable alphabet.

Steven is delighted and asks for new words following the completion of the activity. Ms. Kate gives him a camera to take a picture of his completed work, minimizing the need to write each word. After only a month, Steven begins to read short-vowel early-reading books.

After this activity, the moveable alphabet is presented with photo cards depicting a CVC object. The child takes a card and says the name of the object in the photo. Then, the child makes the sound of each letter and finds the matching letter in the moveable alphabet box. For instance, the child selects the photo of a can and says, "can." Then the child says, "can . . . c," looks for the "c" in the moveable alphabet box, and places it under the photo. The child continues by saying, "c . . . a . . . ," looks for the "a" in the moveable alphabet box, and places it under the photo. He does this until he has completed the word "c . . . a . . . n" and placed all letters below the photo.

The moveable alphabet activity provides consistent and meaningful exposure to symbols by providing the opportunity to match sounds to their visual graphic symbols. Once the child knows a few letters, he discovers that blending the sounds for these symbols forms words, thus beginning cognitive preparation for decoding.[45] This accomplishment aligns explicitly with the UDL Checkpoint 2.2: "Clarify vocabulary and symbols" (Principle of Representation, Guideline 2: Language and Symbols).[46]

EXERCISES FOR READING

Because young children need many opportunities to hear and understand spoken language in order to prepare them to become readers and writers, the Montessori EC program exposes them to a variety of classroom materials across the curriculum. In this way, the Montessori EC program provides "plans and materials for supporting early literacy through reading, learning letters and sounds, writing, and immersion in a print-rich environment" (NAEYC Standard 2, Section E: Early Literacy).[47]

Dr. Montessori believed that children are fascinated by the sounds of language.[48] She also noted that reading demands extensive guided instruction and requires more complex intellectual development. Reading is part of an abstract intellectual culture that is essentially decoded graphic symbols.[49] Accordingly, Dr. Montessori created several activities that she called "Games for Reading" to introduce reading to young children.[50] These games aim to allow children to experience how written words relate to spoken words and to the corresponding objects.

One of these games, The Object Box, contains attractive, miniature items, each with a matching label card. This material conveys an understanding of the written symbol matched to an object. The miniature items provide a visual representation of the word while teaching vocabulary and symbols, which connects to the learners' experience and prior knowledge.[51] The child finds clarity in the visual representations and develops an understanding of "the syntactic or structural relationships between elements of meaning."[52]

A small chest of drawers, always located on the Montessori EC language shelf, is available for the child to use independently after a lesson has been given. Each drawer contains miniature objects and matching small cards bearing the phonetic word naming each object. The cards are classified by spelling patterns and sounds.

In this first lesson, the label cards provide children the opportunity to read phonetic words.[53] The child no longer sees the objects as toys but as miniature objects that have names he can read on the matching cards. The written words arouse his interest.[54]

Modification Example 5: Jonathan is a new 6-year-old child in a Montessori EC classroom. He has some delayed language development and struggles with limited vocabulary and comprehension. Ms. Kate gives him a lesson with the CVC phonics miniature objects and label cards. He carefully attends and is attracted to the objects. Jonathan works diligently each day with the exercise, matching the word on the label to the moveable letter word as he reads it.

After a week, Ms. Kate replaces the objects with photographs of the objects, and Jonathan remembers the object. He looks at the photo of a bat and says to the teacher, "This is a bat. The bat you play baseball with . . . I can find the word 'bat, b . . . a . . . t . . .' I found it!" He picks up the label and places it under the photo.

Another reading activity uses the nomenclature cards, of which there are three kinds: a photo card with the word written below, a photo card without label, and a card with the label only. The game of matching word symbols to photos of objects presents the child with concrete manipulatives for meaning and vocabulary.[55] This activity captures the child's inner drive. She becomes eager to repeat this exercise with other card sets.[56] Nomenclature cards afford children the opportunity to engage with a given word or concept that may be phonetic or non-phonetic (e.g., labeling the parts of the plant with nomenclature cards).

Through partnering and small group work, children learn to communicate meaning and build understanding of vocabulary through conversations.[57] The beautiful nature of working with miniature objects gives the child opportunity to explore and discover. The child has discretion and autonomy to decide to work alone or with peers, an approach that aligns with two UDL guidelines: "Optimize individual choice and autonomy" (Principle of Engagement, Guideline 7: Recruiting Interest, Checkpoint 7.1) and "Promote understanding across languages" (Principle of Representation, Guideline 2: Language and Symbols, Checkpoint 2.4).[58]

Later, when the explosion of writing has occurred, the command cards are presented. The command cards allow children to read sentences that give instruction or direction to do an activity. The command cards are arranged in a rectangular upright box. The teacher selects a card and hands it to the child. The child reads it and completes the action. For example, the following sentence is written on one card: "Open the blinds and turn off the classroom lights." The child silently walks to the window, opens the blinds, walks to the light switch, and turns the classroom lights off.

This exercise allows the child to engage in reading sentences, hence, demonstrating "that composition should precede the rational reading of sentences, just as writing precedes the reading of words. Further, reading that communicates ideas" has a more significant impact when it is done as a mental activity rather than a vocal one.[59]

The extensive three-year literacy journey in the Montessori EC classroom environment grants the child the opportunity to understand that blending sounds forms words, which are symbols representing meaning, and that these symbols are used in reading and writing.[60]

The vast array of EC Montessori language materials provides opportunities for children to engage in multiple activities and exercises that foster communication and expression, organization and classification, and the development of thought. A finely woven tapestry of literacy throughout the curriculum offers the child the means to view language as an instrument of communication with others all over the world. They discover that the written word can convey thoughts and ideas across any distance.

This chapter is a skeletal presentation of Montessori lesson preparation for various groups of students in the area of language acquisition. The wide array of practices in the EC Montessori language curriculum with UDL adaptations can help all children enhance the language skills they learned at home. The Montessori EC language lessons allow children—whether they have learning challenges or not—to enhance their spoken language and to explore the written forms of language. These experiences lay the foundation for literacy and comprehension on the elementary level.[61]

Established 120 years ago, Montessori theory on language education aligns directly with current NAEYC and UDL practices that advocate equity in all EC programs. Early literacy is the catalyst enabling all children to become fully articulate—expressing themselves through writing and acquiring the foundations of early reading with ease. Early literacy is a window that opens, allowing comprehension of the world and the thoughts of others to enter.[62]

EARLY LANGUAGE AND LITERACY ADAPTATIONS AND ALIGNMENT

Table 5.1.

Montessori Material	Lesson Adaption/Alignment	UDL Guidelines
NAEYC Standard 2D: Language Development		
Object in the Environment Nomenclature What is Missing? Object to Object	• The child works with a partner to share their understanding & knowledge of the new vocabulary obtained in the lesson • Through use of language, children express & communicate with each other. • The child learns to match words to objects. • The activities provide concrete manipulatives for meaning & vocabulary. (Montessori, 1988, 236–237)	*Principle*: Action & Expression *Guideline 5*: Expression & Communication, Checkpoint 5.3
Things That Go Together	• The activity provides additional vocabulary support as the child's hands & eyes are attracted to objects, enticing the child to repeat the lesson multiple times. • The activity aids in classification of the environment & development of spoken language. • Allowing the child to work with a partner enables communication of meaning & understanding through conversations. (Montessori, 1988, 237)	*Principle*: Representation & Engagement *Guideline 8*: Sustaining Effort & Persistence, Checkpoint 8.3
NAEYC Standard 2C: Physical Development		
Geometric Metal Insets	• The metal inset allows children to see the shapes & their contours with precision while developing their fine motor skills.	*Principle*: Representation *Guideline 1*: Perception, Checkpoint 1.3
Sandpaper Letters	• By tracing the sandpaper letters, the child receives a sensory-motor stimulus with the mechanical formation of each letter as well as a visual representation of the letter symbol. • A contemporary set of letters can be created by adding lines to an additional set. The placement of the lines will enable the student to see each part of the letter in relationship to the lines. • Rather than using the usual sandpaper letters surrounded by a smooth wooden surface, create a letter set in which smooth wooden letters are surrounded by a sandpaper outline. When tracing the letter shapes, students with sensory challenges will be experiencing the letter shapes from both the rough sand edge of the letters and the smooth surface of the letters. • Tracing letter shapes with the finger helps children prepare to manage a writing instrument.	*Principle*: Representation *Guideline 2*: Language & Symbols, Checkpoint 2.1

Montessori Material	Lesson Adaption/Alignment	UDL Guidelines
	NAEYC Standard 2E: Early Literacy	
Sandpaper Letters	• As the letter is traced while the name of the letter is spoken, the child learns to associate the sound with the shape of each letter, thus preparing the child to read.	*Principle*: Representation *Guideline 2*: Language & Symbols, Checkpoint 2.2
Moveable Alphabet	• Using the moveable alphabet demonstrates to the child that words can be formed when visual recognition of each letter and its sound are associated. • The moveable alphabet provides consistent and meaningful graphic symbols for sound. The coloring of the letters (blue for consonants, red for vowels) helps to emphasize the two letter groups. (Montessori, 1988, 198)	*Principle*: Representation *Guideline 2*: Language & Symbols, Checkpoint 2.2
Games for Reading: Object Box with Labels	• Reading activities allow the child to realize how written words relate to spoken words and the corresponding objects in a fun and attractive way. • The miniature items provide visual representation for the word while teaching vocabulary and symbols, thus connecting the learners' experience and prior knowledge. (Montessori, 1988, 198) • The attractive nature of working with miniature objects is an opportunity for the child to explore and discover. The child has discretion and autonomy to work alone or with a peer. (Montessori, 1965, 145)	*Principle*: Engagement *Guideline 7*: Recruiting Interest, Checkpoint 7.1
Nomenclature: Three-Part Cards	• Using the nomenclature cards helps children name early impressions of the world while classifying the words into simple spelling patterns. • The nomenclature cards allow children to match word symbols to objects. They provide concrete manipulatives for meaning and vocabulary. (Montessori, 1988, 236–237)	*Principle*: Representation *Guideline 2*: Language & Symbols, Checkpoint 2.4
Command Cards	• Command cards allow children to understand how written words relate to spoken words and their corresponding actions.	*Principle*: Representation *Guideline 2*: Language & Symbols, Checkpoint 2.4

NOTES

1. David Gordon, Anne Meyer, and David H. Rose. *Universal Design for Learning: Theory and Practice*, first edition (Wakefield, MA: CAST Professional Publishing, 2014).

2. Every Student Succeeds Act, Congress.gov, 2019, https://congress.gov/114/plaws/publ95/PLAW-114publ95.pdf.

3. "About Universal Design for Learning," CAST.org, 2018, accessed October 15, 2019, http://www.cast.org/our-work/about-udl.html#.Xc9SXDJKigw.#.Xc9SXDJKigw.

4. Maria Montessori, *The Absorbent Mind* (Amsterdam: Clio Press, 1988), 110–15.

5. Paula Polk Lillard and Lynn Lillard Jessen, *Montessori from the Start* (New York: Schocken Books, 2008), 164–65.

6. Ibid., 160–70.

7. Ibid., 166.

8. Maria Montessori, *What You Should Know about Your Child* (Amsterdam: Montessori-Pierson Publishing, 2007), 27.

9. Lillard and Lillard Jessen, *Montessori from the Start*, 162–70.

10. Montessori, *What You Should Know about Your Child*, 29.

11. Montessori, *The Absorbent Mind*, 252–61.

12. Maria Montessori, *Dr. Montessori's Own Handbook: A Short Guide to Her Ideas and Materials* (New York: Schocken Books, 1965), 123–31.

13. Ibid., 123–39.

14. Ibid., 123–24.

15. Ibid., 126.

16. Ibid., 137–38.

17. "NAEYC Early Learning Program Accreditation Standards and Assessment Items," NAEYC.org, July 1, 2019, 10–11, accessed October 8, 2019, https://www.naeyc.org/sites/default/files/globally-shared/downloads/PDFs/accreditation/early-learning/naeyc_elp_accreditation_standards_and_assessment_items_2019.pdf.

18. Peter Dewitz et al., *Teaching Reading in the 21st Century: Motivating All Learners*, fifth edition (Hoboken, NJ: Pearson Education, 2010), 2–8.

19. "NAEYC Early Learning Program Accreditation Standards and Assessment Items," 10–11.

20. Paula Polk Lillard, *Montessori: A Modern Approach* (New York: Schocken Books, 1972), 120–37.

21. Ibid., 123–31.

22. Graves, Michael F., and Susan Watts-Taffe. "For the Love of Words: Fostering Word Consciousness in Young Readers," *Reading Teacher* 62, no. 3

(International Literacy Association and Wiley, 2008), 185–93, www.jstor.org/stable/20143930.

23. Maria Montessori, *The Discovery of the Child* (Amsterdam: Clio Press, 1988), 231–41.

24. "About Universal Design for Learning."

25. Montessori, *Dr. Montessori's Own Handbook*, 131–34; "CAST: About Universal Design for Learning."

26. Ibid.

27. Lillard, *Montessori*, 120–34.

28. "About Universal Design for Learning."

29. Montessori, *Dr. Montessori's Own Handbook*, 146.

30. "NAEYC Early Learning Program Accreditation Standards and Assessment Items," 10–11.

31. Montessori, *The Absorbent Mind*, 125–35.

32. Montessori, *Dr. Montessori's Own Handbook*, 139.

33. Ibid., 140–48.

34. Ibid.

35. Ibid., 143–48.

36. "About Universal Design for Learning."

37. Montessori, *Dr. Montessori's Own Handbook*, 144–47.

38. "About Universal Design for Learning."

39. "NAEYC Early Learning Program Accreditation Standards and Assessment Items," 10–11.

40. Montessori, *Dr. Montessori's Own Handbook*, 148–53.

41. Ibid., 148–152.

42. Montessori, *The Discovery of the Child,* 213.

43. "About Universal Design for Learning."

44. Montessori, *Dr. Montessori's Own Handbook*, 153–54.

45. "About Universal Design for Learning," 198.

46. "About Universal Design for Learning."

47. "NAEYC Early Learning Program Accreditation Standards and Assessment Items," 10–11.

48. Montessori, *The Absorbent Mind,* 105–15.

49. Montessori, *The Discovery of the Child*, 230–42.

50. Ibid., 232.

51. Ibid., 230–32.

52. "About Universal Design for Learning."

53. Lillard, *Montessori*, 131.

54. Montessori, *The Discovery of the Child*, 231–33.

55. Ibid., 232–37.

56. Lillard, *Montessori*, 132–35.

57. Montessori, *The Discovery of the Child*, 238–40.
58. "About Universal Design for Learning."
59. Montessori, *The Discovery of the Child*, 240.
60. Lillard, *Montessori*, 120–37.
61. Montessori, *The Discovery of the Child*, 241–42.
62. Ibid., 186–203.

BIBLIOGRAPHY

CAST. *Universal Design for Learning Guidelines Version 2.2*, 2018. Accessed October 15, 2019. http://udlguidelines.cast.org.

Dewitz, Peter, Michael F. Graves, Connie F. Juel, and Bonnie B. Graves, *Teaching Reading in the 21st Century: Motivating All Learners*, fifth edition. Hoboken, NJ: Pearson Education, 2010.

Every Student Succeeds Act of 2015, Pub. L. No. 114-95, 129 STAT. 1802 (2015). Accessed October 15, 2019. https://congress.gov/114/plaws/publ95/PLAW-114publ95.pdf.

Gordon, David, Anne Meyer, and David H. Rose. *Universal Design for Learning: Theory and Practice*, first edition. Wakefield, MA: CAST Professional Publishing, 2014.

Graves, Michael F., and Watts-Taffe, Susan. "For the Love of Words: Fostering Word Consciousness in Young Readers." *Reading Teacher* 62, no. 3 (2008): 185–93. Accessed November 4, 2019. www.jstor.org/stable/20143930.

Lillard, Paula Polk. *Montessori: A Modern Approach*. New York: Schocken Books, 1972.

Lillard, Paula Polk, and Lynn Lillard Jessen. *Montessori from the Start: A Child at Home, from Birth to Age Three*. New York: Schocken Books, 2008.

Montessori, Maria. *Dr. Montessori's Own Handbook: A Short Guide to Her Ideas and Materials*. New York: Schocken Books, 1965.

Montessori, Maria. *The Discovery of the Child*. Amsterdam: Clio Press, 1988.

Montessori, Maria. *The Absorbent Mind*. Amsterdam: Clio Press, 1988.

Montessori, Maria. *What You Should Know about Your Child*. Amsterdam: Montessori-Pierson Publishing, 2007.

National Association for the Education of Young Children. "NAEYC Early Learning Program Accreditation Standards and Assessment Items." NAEYC.org, July 1, 2019. Accessed October 8, 2019. https://www.naeyc.org/sites/default/files/globally-shared/downloads/PDFs/accreditation/early-learning/naeyc_elp_accreditation_standards_and_assessment_items_2019.pdf.

Conclusion
Ginger Kelley McKenzie and Victoria S. Zascavage

This book was written to support teachers in Montessori early childhood classrooms who have children with challenges. Its aim is not so much to describe how materials function in the Montessori classroom but rather the ways the materials and philosophy of Maria Montessori can be adapted to accommodate children with a variety of learning styles.

Maria Montessori, a twentieth-century visionary, designed a program to educate students with intellectual disabilities. Because of the contemporary nature of our interpretation of Montessori, we have designed this book to use twenty-first-century expertise to accommodate students in early childhood Montessori classrooms. The methods and use of concrete materials are not exclusive to Montessori and are suited for incorporation into any traditional classroom that needs additional pedagogical support for students to learn.

Specifically, the chapters in this book have recommended accommodations for traditional Montessori lessons on how to adjust or represent these lessons to children with learning challenges. Many lessons adhere to the principles of Universal Design for Learning (UDL) and the specific standards from the National Association for the Education of Young Children (NAEYC) and apply these principles to specific Montessori lessons for children aged 3 to 6 in the areas of Practical Life, Sensorial Lessons, Mathematics, and Language Arts.

The goal of an adapted Montessori curriculum is to welcome all students into a full Montessori experience. For the students who need additional support, the joy of learning depends on a prepared environment designed to maximize their active participation. The foundation curriculum, designed by Maria Montessori and adapted in this book, employs concrete materials of beauty and purpose to engage all students in learning through a cherished experience. Based on the pedagogy of Maria Montessori and modernized by the guidelines of the NAEYC and UDL, this book encompasses the perspective of five authors with many years of experience in Montessori early childhood and/or special education who bring their expertise to chronicle the new Montessori normal.

PRACTICAL LIFE CHAPTER

Practical Life Activities include: Ground Rules, Grace and Courtesy, Control of Movement, Care of the Environment, and Care of Self. Teacher presentations of Practical Life Lessons, carried out with care and enthusiasm and involving analysis of movement and simple-to-complex procedure, develop students' love for work and for the environment. Young children—with and without challenges—gradually become calm, more orderly, more independent, and develop an improved attention span and strengthened concentration. The child's eye-hand coordination also becomes more developed. The benefits of Practical Life are evident in the joyful and peaceful Montessori environment.

A teacher in coauthor My Le Vo's school commented that thanks to Practical Life activities, the student with attention deficit hyperactivity disorder could gradually slow down and complete the work at hand. It was as though the student became a new child—calmer, more comfortable, happier, and more focused.

Montessori methods enable all students, whether with or without challenges, to achieve a steady, continuous acquisition of orderliness, concentration, coordination, and independence. It is this that helps young learners develop confidence and enjoyment of learning, thus ensuring their success in future academic endeavors.

As the children—including those who need additional support—actively work with Practical Life lessons, they strengthen their gross and fine motor skills and enhance their balance and coordination. Educators understand that developed eye-hand coordination is essential in future reading and writing activities. As the child observes the teacher's careful presentations of lessons and subsequently works to complete each lesson, he or she develops a deepening joy of learning. In this way, young learners gradually acquire good work habits, inner discipline, and a growing sense of self-esteem.

SENSORIAL CHAPTER

The Sensorial Curriculum in a Montessori classroom is unique and has been developed with specific aims to support children's development. This chapter describes those aims, outlines the specific qualities of the materials, and provides examples of both the materials and ways that they can be adapted to meet the needs of both typically developing children and children with challenges.

The lessons given by the teacher are brief and practical and begin with concrete materials that the child can explore using sensorial methods. The introductory lesson given by the teacher demonstrates how children with and without challenges can successfully interact with the materials. With the child, the teacher demonstrates each step of the process, from fetching and unrolling a work rug to carrying the exercise to the rug. Depending on the child's interest and attention, the teacher can complete a full presentation, from beginning to end, or can engage the child in the process.

Following the presentation, the child is free to work with the material, repeat the presentation, and explore various ways to do the work. Through each hands-on experience, the child is both mentally and physically engaged, working independently and developing increasing concentration, order, and coordination.

The process of abstraction is individual, slow, and related to brain development and the child's experience. It helps those who have challenges and those without challenges. As educators, we often try to hurry the process for external purposes. Also, adults are so comfortable functioning in the abstract that teachers often make the mistake of thinking that if a teacher simply tells the child a fact and the child can repeat it to the teacher, it means the child has mastered it abstractly. But that is memorization, and memorization alone does not help the child in learning and understanding.

Abstraction cannot be taught; it depends on the child's development, experiences within the environment, and mental maturity. Immersing the child in sensorial experiences with materials that are concrete, ordered, sequenced, complete, and mathematically designed will provide the child with experiences and time to move from sensation to perception. Then, when he or she is ready, the child will move on to conceptual understanding.

All activities in this sensory area are purposeful, with specific educational aims that can be varied to respond to individual interests, developmental levels, and needs.

The direct aim of all the sensorial materials is the education and refinement of the senses. Indirectly, each material supports the development of both math and language concepts. The mathematical concept inherent in the Pink Tower is discrimination of volume. The direct aim is the refinement of the visual sense of dimension so that, through repetition, the child can see increasingly subtle differences.

The Sensorial curriculum area contains materials that support the education and refinement of all the senses by all children, including those children who have challenges. The materials are placed on open shelves in sequential order. While most of the materials are multisensory, they are arranged on the shelves according to the primary sense that the material is designed to teach to.

MATH CHAPTER

Within the Montessori math program, preparation of the classroom promotes instructional regulation and creates an opportunity for routine, both of which lead to independence. Classroom preparation also enables all children to learn as they become familiar with the materials for math and geometry, which naturally encompass the lessons learned in Practical Life and Sensorial. For the student who needs additional support to assist with attention deficit disorder, autism, or developmental delay, this book describes strategies and materials common to the Montessori classroom and correlated with the principles of UDL.

In the Montessori classroom, the Prepared Environment is a critical component of early mathematical learning. The environment in the Montessori classroom is prepared to allow the child to absorb knowledge by immersion in a progression of mathematical activities that follows a specific order, building from simple to complex.

The aim of the Prepared Environment initially presented in the Practical Life lessons is to create independence, a sense of ownership of the task at hand, and an overall growing sense of self-efficacy. The teacher quietly keeps watch and writes observation notes about each child. He is looking for obstacles that may inhibit the child's ability to become an independent learner.

Maria Montessori encouraged the concept of exploration to engage the curiosity of all children, including those who need additional support. This concept still has merit in the twenty-first-century concept of special education. Students with certain exceptionalities may need a more structured introduction to engage in the exploration of the Prepared Environment.

The Prepared Environment helps guide the immature learner and the student who needs additional support to find calm, order, and safety in the learning activity. Order in the environment creates predictability and safety in repetition and conserves intellectual and physical energy. In a well-prepared mathematical environment, everything has a designated space. This creates the sense of security that is so important in an inclusive classroom.

For the child with a developmental delay and for others who have not demonstrated the ability to initiate the sequence, picture prompts facilitate independence by assisting short-term memory. The picture prompts should be phased out gradually as the child shows she can do the activity without these prompts. If children have responded positively to picture-based visual prompts, the use of picture prompts is also suggested for those on the autism spectrum,. Picture cards are two sided. On one side is a photograph of the step to take (e.g., a child pouring water into a container); on the other side is the summative word "pour."

Sensorial and Practical Life activities and Number Ordering activities are going on simultaneously; they are not progressive or exclusionary. The three intertwine to allow the child to experience early number concepts in mathematics. The Montessori early childhood mathematical curriculum builds on already known relationships and sequence.

Any change in material may elicit difficulties for children who need additional support. Generalizing previous learnings so they can be applied to new lessons rarely happens spontaneously for these students, and the issue must be addressed before proceeding. A detailed explanation of the relationship of new material to a previously mastered skill must be provided to students with challenges

Teachers should refrain from using words such as "left-hand bottom corner" or "this half of the rug" when giving instructions to students who need addition support because this verbiage presents a dual relationship that may confuse the child. The child should be able to focus on the rod activity and not on description of placement. For this reason, teachers model the concept without extraneous vocabulary. The repetition and predictability of the First Step can be beneficial for the child with autism who is comfortable with routine.

Repetition of an unsuccessful experience can create learned helplessness, particularly for a child with learning challenges. Therefore, sensitivity to the success of the child is critical.

The student who needs additional support may need to build up to completing the full Ten Rod Activity. However, after mastery of the Number Rods 1–4, the instructor should determine if the student is capable of going through all ten rods before moving onto the Second Period Lesson of the Number Rod and Smooth Numeral Card Activity. If the student demonstrates mastery of Number Rods 1-4 has been accomplished but movement to Number Rods 5–9 is creating a source of frustration, then the student should move through the Third Period Lesson with only Number Rods 1–4.

Just as the Sensorial and Practical Life activities are going on while the child learns his or her beginning number concepts, early geometric concepts are also being explored in the early childhood Montessori environment. The lessons in this chapter provide examples of how the teacher should proceed with early math lessons, taking into consideration the need for differentiation of presentation and assessment for students who need additional support.

Maria Montessori was the first true special educator. In the early 1900s, her methods of instruction in mathematics used differentiated instruction and placed students who needed additional support side by side with their typical peers. Montessori math teachers have instructional strategies that are time tested and universal. These strategies promote learning for student who needs additional support, just as they do for students who do not have specific challenges.

LANGUAGE CHAPTER

The previously forgotten, challenged, and disabled children of our society are no longer isolated. Now they are part of the rich mosaic student population in general classrooms around the world. In the public education sector, the ratio of children needing additional support continues to increase as educational systems worldwide work hard to integrate all general education classrooms, providing new training and resources and setting high expectations for learning outcomes. Montessori teachers, like many others in early childhood education, wrestle with facilitating instruction for students with a wide assortment of needs.

The language chapter serves as a guide in preparing Montessori lessons for a diverse group of learners in the area of language development.

Maria Montessori believed that babies obtain language in careful observation of their natural environment. The baby absorbs language from the womb. Simple names of objects and activities that are heard lay the foundations for intellectual interaction with what is happening. After the acquisition of substantive words (nouns), the child launches into the use of all kinds of words (verbs, prepositions, adjectives, or adverbs), which prepares the child for speaking and writing sentences.

Dr. Montessori wanted to take advantage of this absorption of language in the Early Childhood classroom. Hence, she created a rich, prepared environment with which to surround the child. She designed the materials and gave strong directives for implementing classroom environments.

Dr. Montessori believed that children must understand the materials in their environment. That knowledge is obtained through various motor explorations and sensorial experiences. The foundation of language is built through the senses of sight, hearing, touch, taste, and smell. Montessori's methods help the child learn, sort, classify, and store information about his or her environment in an orderly fashion.

In Montessori classrooms, language development begins with the initial lesson in practical life and sensorial lessons. Later, it is woven into all areas of the curriculum. Through various exercises in practical life and sensorial lessons, the child prepares the mind and the hand. Listening, talking, reading, and writing are all parts of early literacy learning and are connected wonderfully in the Montessori Early Childhood classroom.

Dr. Montessori created a set of sandpaper alphabets that include both lower- and uppercase letters of the alphabet. Two colors of wooden card boards hold the tan sandpaper letters: Each vowel is in a blue board; each consonant in pink. The sandpaper letters serve multiple objectives: They provide the visual recognition of letters, the kinesthetic recognition of letters and the phonetic sound of letters and they train the hand for the light touch needed for writing.

Dr. Montessori also designed a green phonogram set to teach the various letter symbols that represent different sounds. The phonograms are presented to children when they demonstrate readiness to learn them.

In the Montessori EC classroom environment, the moveable alphabet is used to introduce the child to building words, thoughts, and sentences with graphic symbols—even if the hand is not ready to write with a pencil. The objective of this material is to show the child that words are formed by matching visual recognition of letters to sounds. The letters are graphic symbols for sounds. The sandpaper letter cards were blue (vowels) and pink (consonants), and the moveable alphabet letters themselves are blue and pink. Because vowels are one color and consonants are another, the child learns that the letters of each color form a group within the alphabet.

The moveable alphabet is presented with cards showing a photograph of an object (such as a cat) and spelling the name of the object (c-a-t). The child takes a card and says the name of the pictured object. Then the child speaks each letter sound, finds the matching letter in the moveable alphabet box, and uses the letter to make the word on the table. The moveable alphabet provides consistent and meaningful exposure to symbols by using the visual graphic objects to identify sounds.

Young children need many opportunities to hear and understand spoken language. The vast array of Montessori CE language materials provides opportunities for children to engage in multiple activities/exercises that foster communication and expression, organization and classification, and the development of thought. A tapestry of vocabulary woven throughout the curriculum offers the child a means of viewing language as an instrument of communication with others. They discover that the written word conveys thoughts and ideas.

This chapter provided a skeletal structure for preparation of language acquisition lessons for diverse groups of students in Montessori classrooms. The Montessori EC language lessons allow all children, regardless of their learning challenges, to enhance their spoken language and explore written forms of language. Montessori theory on language education from 120 years ago aligns directly with the prominent NAEYC and UDL practices advocating equity in all early childhood programs.

Appendix

Montessori Early Childhood Principles and Applications

Principle	*Application*
Prepared Environment	To understand and provide for the child's developmental needs, the child needs an environment that responds to those specific needs. The needs will grow and change as the child goes through Montessori Planes of Development. Montessori: *"The first aim of the prepared environment is, as far as it possible, to render the growing child independent of the adult. That is, it is a place where (they) can do things for (themselves) without the immediate help of adults"* (Standing, 1962, 267).
Observation	Adults can learn children's needs and interests by observing them and adapting/adjusting the environment. Children learn holistically, so the environment must respond to the whole child (cognitive, social, emotional, physical, and spiritual). Through observation, the teacher prepares and maintains the environment and assists children connect to the activities and materials in the environment. Montessori: *"We should start observing the child when (their) senses begin to accumulate conscious impressions of the external world, since it is then that a life is spontaneously developing at the expense of its environment"* (1979, 47).
Freedom within Limits	Children need freedom to explore within the prepared environment. The only limits that are to be placed relate to safety and respect: for the child, for others, and for the environment. It is not abandonment ("I don't care what you do.") or anarchy ("Do whatever you want."), but rather is a result of the child's development and numerous opportunities to make choices and experience the consequences of those choices.

Principle	Application
	Montessori: *"The first thing I particularly noticed was a little girl of about three busy slipping cylinders in and out of their containers. These cylinders are of different sizes and have corresponding holes into which they fit like a cork in a bottle. I began to count and she repeated the exercise forty-two times. Then she stopped as if coming out of a dream and smiled happily"* (1979, 119).
Role of the Teacher	The Montessori teacher does not take on the traditional role of teacher but is more like a guide. Primary roles include observation, preparation of the environment, and connecting each child with materials in the environment. The teacher collaborates with families. *Montessori listed special circumstances which identify the role of the teacher and allow for a pleasant Montessori environment, including (1) a clean classroom, (2) "special materials with which to work and teach the children how to concentrate," and (3) the importance of teachers remaining calm. "This calm consists in a spiritual humility and intellectual purity necessary for (the teachers) to understand each child"* (1979, 137).
Absorbent Mind & Sensitive Periods (First Plane of Development)	From birth until six years, children learn in a way very different from adults. They absorb information/experiences from the environment (sensory/motor), and experience sensitive or critical periods. Children are best served when the environment is rich in experiences that respond and support the special sensitivities. An example is the sensitive period for language. Montessori: *"Children pass through definite periods in which they reveal psychic aptitudes and possibilities which afterwards disappear. During such a period the child is endowed with a special sensibility which urges (them) to focus (their) attention on certain aspects of (the) environment to the exclusion of others"* (1979, 120).
Development of Community	Community is supported by children's ownership and responsibility for the environment. Everything is geared to their needs and interests. The children are encouraged to care for the environment and show respect to visitors. Children of different ages are included in the environment. For early childhood, the children enter at age three and remain in the same classroom for three years, with the same teachers. Ideally, only one third of the class moves on each year. Cooperation is encouraged rather than competition. Each child is honored for the specific interests and strengths that they bring to the class. Children move freely in the environment and interact with other children in a natural, spontaneous manner. Younger children see older children engaged in cognitively challenging activities and visualize themselves doing that as they get older.

Appendix

Principle	Application
	Montessori: *"I have come to appreciate the fact that children have a deep sense of personal dignity. When visitors came to the school, the children behaved with dignity and self-respect. They know how to receive these visitors with warm enthusiasm and show them how they carried out their tasks"* (1979, 126–127).
Self-Discipline	Montessori believed that by giving freedom, children developed inner or self-discipline. To support this approach, materials are self-correcting and children are active in choice making. They are also responsible for their own actions (cleaning up spilled water, comforting an injured child). Montessori: *"The peaceful atmosphere that pervaded the classroom as the children pursued their work was extremely touching. No one had provoked it, and no one could have obtained it by external means. They worked quietly, each one intent on (their) own particular occupation"* (1979, 129–130).
Meaningful Work & Independence	Montessori called the children's activities "'work'" since she saw their self-chosen activities as a way that they construct themselves. All activities are designed to be done independently. Montessori notes that during Practical Life exercises, *"one child sweeps the floor, another polishes brass items, and a third puts fresh water in flower vases. These exercises are important for the children to develop independence and responsibility for their environment"* (Standing, 1962, 213).
Concentration	When children select activities that are of interest to them, they develop the ability to focus on a task from start to finish. This focus supports future learning. Montessori: *"Despite their easy freedom of manner, the children on the whole gave the impression of being extraordinarily disciplined. They worked quietly, each one intent on (their) own particular occupation"* (1979, 129).
Order	Order is an important goal for children. Not compulsive order, but rather an internalization of order in how an activity is completed, order within social interactions, and physical order (motor planning). In addition, order within routines supports children in their ability to predict and plan their activities. Montessori: *"They (the children) quietly walked to and from as they took or replaced the objects with which they worked"* (1979, 129). And *"What particularly fascinated visitors was the order and discipline they managed to combine with spontaneity"* (1979, 130).
Free choice	Children may choose to work with any material in the environment and keep the materials as long as needed. They may choose to work alone or invite another child. Repetition is important as children internalize and deepen their knowledge and understanding.

Principle	Application
	Montessori: *"The children arranged their day as they pleased. They would take the objects they wanted for their work, and then tidy up the school. If the teacher came late or left the children alone, everything went on just as well"* (1979, 130).
Limited Materials	In most cases, Montessori environment will include only one of each material. This supports the development of self-discipline, since the child's immediate choice may not be available. However, there are hundreds of other activities that the child may choose until that activity is available. The child soon learns that the rule also protects them when they have an activity in which they are deeply involved. Materials are never removed from the environment while a child's interest continues.
	Montessori: *"Even the materials themselves are beautiful: witness the color tablets with their sixty-three different shades, the ten different colors in the bead stairs (numbers 1 to 10), shining golden decimal system beads; the bright grammar symbols, etc"* (Standing, 1962, 268).
Self-correcting Materials	Most of the materials include a way for children to see if they have made an error. The goal is for them to become able to monitor their activities and adjust/adapt them when they don't work. This is NOT to prevent errors, since we all learn from our errors. The materials are designed to interest children at increasingly complex cognitive levels. Teachers acknowledge children's accomplishments without praise.
	Montessori *"has also brought into being a 'new teacher' and she used the name 'directress' because the primary function is not so much to teach as to direct a natural energy in the children"* (Standing, 1962, 297) *who are engaged in the self-correcting activities.*
Initiative	The environment provides a long work cycle in which to choose activities, decide how long to work with them and with whom to work. Teachers support children by either expanding or limiting choices to help children in the development of initiative.
	Montessori: *"We should aim at helping children to help themselves; enabling them in every emergency to act independently of the adult—thus becoming masters of their environment and conscious of their power over it. If someone upsets a vase of flowers, a child is already prepared to fetch a pail and cloth and mop up the water"* (Standing, 1962, 216).
Attachment	Children stay in the same learning environment with the same teachers and (mostly) the same children for three years, supporting strong social and emotional bonds.

Principle	Application
	Montessori: *"The Children's House has a two-fold importance: the social importance which it assumes through its peculiarity of being a school within the house (for ages 3 to 6), and its purely pedagogic importance gained through its methods for the education of very young children"* who enjoy working together for often three years (1964, 44).
Movement	Montessori believed that, in order to learn, children needed to move and be physically involved in the process. Therefore, in a Montessori environment, children are actively and physically engaged with the materials, using both fine and gross movement. The connection and involvement of the hand and the mind is essential.
	Montessori: *"The importance of physical activity or movement in psychic development should be emphasized. A child develops through personal effort and engagement. His growth, therefore, depends upon psychic as well as physical factors"* (1979, 96).

RESOURCES

Lillard, Angeline Stoll. *Montessori, The Science Behind the Genius.* New York: Oxford University Press, 2005.
Lillard, Paula Polk. *Montessori: A Modern Approach.* New York: Schochken Books, 1972.
Montessori, Maria. *The Montessori Method.* New York: Schocken Books, 1964.
Montessori, Maria. *Maria Montessori: The Secret of Childhood.* New York: Ballantine Books, 1979.
Seldin, Tim, and Paul Epstein. *The Montessori Way.* Bradenton, FL: Montessori Foundation Press, *2003.*
Standing, E. M. *Maria Montessori: Her Life and Work.* New York: The New American Library of World Literature, 1962.

Compiled by Crystal Dahlmeier, Montessori consultant and lecturer, Greater Cincinnati Center for Montessori Education.

Maria Montessori quotes added by Ginger McKenzie, professor emerita, Xavier University, Cincinnati, Ohio.

About the Authors

Ginger Kelley McKenzie, EdD, is professor emeritus, Montessori Institute, Xavier University, a past member the Board of Directors of the American Montessori Society (2010–2016, and the former executive director at Amarillo Montessori Academy, Amarillo, Texas, where she also taught 3–6, 6–9, and 9–12. Ginger has thirty-nine journal publications and fifty-six professional presentations in the United States, Taiwan, South Korea, and Canada.

Victoria S. Zascavage, PhD, is associate professor and director of special education programs in the School of Education, Xavier University. With a focus on issues of transition, equity, and educational best practices for students, she has published in journals such as the *International Journal of Special Education*, *Teacher Education Quarterly*, *Middle School Journal*, *Higher Education Research and Development*, and *International Journal of Humanities and Social Science*.

Vanessa M. Rigaud, EdD, is assistant professor at the Montessori Institute, Xavier University, in Cincinnati, Ohio, and a former teacher and administrator in both public and private Montessori schools. She holds Montessori credentials in Early Childhood and elementary I–II.

Crystal Dahlmeier, MEd, is a Montessori consultant, teaches at two Montessori teacher-training centers, and holds a Montessori credential in Early Childhood. She has taught in Montessori classrooms in the United

States, the UK, Australia, and South Korea for over forty years. She has presented at conferences both nationally and internationally.

My Le N. Vo, MEd, is the principal and middle school teacher at the Montessori Learning Institute and executive director and instructor at the Montessori Teacher Education Institute, Houston, Texas. She holds a Montessori credential in Early Childhood and elementary. She is the author of various educational materials and teacher-training manuals.

www.ingramcontent.com/pod-product-compliance
Lightning Source LLC
Chambersburg PA
CBHW030143240426
43672CB00005B/248